Leading
for
Change

How to thrive
during uncertain times

Kathryn Simpson

Rethink

Contents

Introduction: A Journey From Scientist To Change Facilitator

I discovered halfway through my career that what I love to do is make change happen so that organisations and teams can achieve their desired future. I've noticed that the key ingredient to making change happen is how it is led, and by working alongside leaders of teams and organisations, I have identified what is critical to make change work.

People ask, 'How did you end up doing this change work?' Each stage of my career created different insights for me. These are the change capabilities I grew during those experiences:

- Analytical chemist – I used step-by-step structured thinking to identify and solve problems.

- Product developer – I made connections with people and listened to cross-functional perspectives to enable change.

- Consultant – I brought value to who I worked with *and* left organisations ready to implement change, focusing on the end goal to get results.

- Internal consultant and department leader – I thought strategically and for the long term, considering the big picture to ensure what was done mattered.

- Independent consultant – I facilitated strategic change, clarified the purpose of organisations and teams to engage people and get results, and saw how using a facilitator allows teams to focus on content – especially useful when times are tough.

As a line manager and an external and internal consultant, I have seen change from different perspectives. This has allowed me to become a facilitator who focuses on the process of change, enabling leaders in organisations to develop a clear pathway to success.

CASE STUDY – CLOSING DOWN AN ORGANISATION

One of the most self-empowered groups I ever worked with was a women's health board of an organisation that was closing down. They had asked me to facilitate a session with them as the government (their only source of funds) had dramatically reduced funding, so they wanted to decide how to use their remaining funds and how to continue their work through other avenues.

About three days before I was due to run the workshop, the government announced that it was withdrawing all its funds. Government representatives wanted to come to the workshop and explain.

Emotions were understandably running high. The meeting, although a tough one, was successful for three main reasons. We:

- Had clearly defined what the outcomes of the meeting were going to be
- Agreed how we were going to behave as a group
- Visibly captured all the discussion points

Having a facilitator who owned this group process and took control was crucial as it enabled the board to focus purely on the content of the discussion, knowing that all their agenda items would be covered and decisions would be recorded so that they wouldn't need to be revisited. The end result of this emotional session was that the group was able to make decisions and move on. The great work that they had done in the past was going to continue via other avenues.

I describe a facilitator as 'enabling meetings to be successful by running the group process, allowing team leaders and participants to focus on the content of the meeting'. This helps to clarify a facilitator vs team-leader role. Implicit within this definition is that a facilitator enables a high quality of conversation and participant engagement, which is crucial to achieving strong buy-in to the outcomes of the meeting.

If you are a team leader, a facilitator frees you up to engage in content discussions, allowing you to advocate your position. A neutral facilitator supports leaders in engaging the group and ensures other perspectives are heard.

In the example above, having a facilitator allowed the group, who knew the challenges they were facing, to address them directly. They did not get tied up with thinking about the process they were using to get to their desired meeting outcome. We will discuss how to decide whether you need to have a facilitator in Chapter 4.

As a leader, it is important to understand your role – when you are going to be a content expert (someone who knows *what* needs to be done) or a facilitator (who focuses on *how* the work needs to get done), or a combination of both roles. Having someone alongside you to provide an objective neutral perspective throughout a change can be invaluable. They help in defining what that change is and how to implement the change.

This is especially valuable in times of uncertainty. It can take change from being overwhelming for an organisation and its leaders, to being empowering.

Each experience I've had in my journey from scientist to change facilitator has been invaluable in building knowledge of leading change as they have each built on a previous experience. There are many paths to facilitating and leading change effectively, so I hope you can make use of my learnings.

Step-by-step process thinking

My journey to leading change had a scientific structural grounding. As a scientist at university, and then as an analytical chemist, I learned to follow a scientific process with my experiments: objective, method, results, conclusion. This is the way scientists work, proving new methods through logic. For me, it was a natural step to shift from scientific methodology to structured business thinking.

The concept of (business) process thinking had its roots in industrial engineering nearly a century ago.[1] It continued to evolve through total quality management, business process reengineering and workflow analysis. Like scientific methodology, each activity completed within the workplace leads to the next until a product or service is delivered. Understanding that your job is just one part of the process to get a product to the end user and appreciating the organisational complexities is the basis of structured systems thinking.

You can use a scientific mindset of logical structured thinking to help the process of change as it provides a neutral objective way to move forward and to reassure those involved, especially if they have scientific, engineering or financial training. Appreciating the organisation-wide view in a structured way is critical in leading effective change as you are able to understand how one change in one part of the organisation can impact other areas.

Making connections

The next stage of my career was as a product developer, a different way of working to my previous experience as an analytical chemist in the laboratory. Part of my role was to troubleshoot products that weren't performing to specification: identifying the causes of issues and, with logical application, persuading others to change their ways of working.

This was highly valued by some of the creative and intuitive colleagues I worked with as they didn't have that skillset, but I was starting to realise that it wasn't just logic that helped people to change, despite the fact that most of the people I was working with were scientists or engineers. I had to do some business learning quickly if I was going to launch new products successfully, which was the main part of my job.

My boss suggested that one of the things I should do on a regular basis was call in to the factory and see how things were going. After all, manufacturing the products that I was developing was the end goal. I have to say, I didn't act on this advice as quickly as I could have, as it seemed a waste of time without having an objective for being in the factory. I was busy enough as it was, but he was the boss, so I decided to create a few objectives.

In retrospect, I realise his wise advice helped me to understand the manufacturing process. Later when I asked my manufacturing colleagues to shut down a production line so that I could perform trials with new products, I already appreciated what an expensive business proposal that was, and one that went against the production department's drive for volume.

Logic, structure and step-by-step process thinking are invaluable, whether you are analysing products, troubleshooting manufacturing processes or improving business processes. You will have a strong base to persuade people to change if the reasons for change are logical. Understanding how what you do impacts others in doing their job will also help you to make a change that works for everyone. This is structured system thinking at its best.

Cross-functional working

As a product developer, I discovered that the only way to get a product to market was to work across many different disciplines and functions. I soon learned that my structured systems thinking was only one ingredient to make change happen. People will only change if they trust you.

If you are influencing people to make change, you need to build relationships. This is critical if you're working across functions. Although I was in research and development (R&D), my role was not just about developing a new product. I had to work with:

- Suppliers to provide technical specifications, and thus my colleagues in purchasing who were responsible for the overall relationship
- Engineers who designed the manufacturing process and the machines in which the product was used

- Manufacturers who turned my product into something that could be produced at volume
- Marketers who did research and positioned the product in the market to create a launch plan
- Sales and customer service people who evaluated what customers thought
- Support services like human resources, finance and office management

This was quite difficult, as instead of working with people who were like me with a structured scientific mindset, I discovered that each individual function had different capabilities and ways of working that contributed to bringing a product to the market. I found new barriers in moving forward because of different personalities. It wasn't always a straight line to success.

By listening to others' perspectives and adapting my style, I helped them to meet ambitious timelines with the right quality product. Bringing people from individual functions together in one room and ensuring we were all clear about what was needed to progress was critical. Personal connections meant a lot and were powerful when combined with logical step-by-step process thinking. The results that we achieved then and the bonds we formed have lasted many years.

Working across functions to lead change needs different people to cooperate to be successful. If you are a leader of change, then understanding the impacts that change has on different people in different functions is critical. Integrating those impacts and creating a common vison and aligned action plan is even more important.

Bringing value

My first days as a consultant were bewildering. Where was the result of my work? It was no longer in the scientific discoveries that I had made. And I couldn't go and look at the factory or new products that had made a difference when I was a product developer. Instead, there was the concept of value: that what I did would eventually make a difference to business results.
It took me a while to find where I was adding value. It wasn't in the amazing report that I masterminded with a group of wonderful analysts and thought leaders. Instead, I found it when I saw client teams creating solutions, and then implementing them to get results. Recognising that people pay me for business results has meant I continue to focus to create actions that will lead to this.

As a change leader, you need a constant focus on the end results. Sometimes it's so easy to get embroiled in applying the latest tool that you lose sight of the end goal. Change becomes change for its own sake.

Resolving challenges in working with various people can divert you away from the end goal. Focusing on the end goal and designing a process that will bring others on the journey in the most effective way is what leads to value. This is just as important for a leader as it is for a consultant.

Strategic thinking

When I moved from an external to an internal consulting role (aka process improvement management), I was immediately assigned to fix a broken process.

I worked on this process with a wonderful team and we made some great changes that improved customer satisfaction and efficiency.

I asked my new boss, 'Why this process? Where does it fit in the strategy?' In response, he asked me to help him develop a long-term strategic plan. With the input of the leadership team, we outlined our key objectives, one of which was to identify the process improvements that would have the most impact based on a number of criteria. We then implemented more impactful process improvements where processes seemed to be working on the surface, but when they were done differently, it had a large positive impact on revenue generation.

The essence of strategic thinking is asking about the bigger picture, often by gathering external information. By getting involved in developing long-range plans, you see strategic thinking in action. You need to challenge the direction that others are setting, ask why and understand the risks and benefits of various options.

Facilitating and leading change

When I started my business in 2007, I wanted to continue my journey of helping leaders to prepare for change. I had learned how to be a strong systems and strategic thinker, worked at bringing cross-functional groups together, and brought value to internal and external clients. It was time to hone each of these skills and transfer them to others whom I worked with while delivering the results they needed.

The journey that I started on many years ago as a structured process thinker has evolved to one of understanding the critical importance of the people side of change and thinking more strategically.

Leading change effectively is important for everyone today. It used to be that leaders could simply direct people to do a job, manage budgets and monitor performance, but if you ever needed to be a good strategic thinker and a great leader of change, that time is now.

There are many reasons why leading change effectively is more important than it has ever been. As I write this, we are in the midst of a global pandemic. Change like we have never seen before has been imposed on us. This change, while truly disruptive, is just one of many that we will experience in our lifetime.

Uncertainties come at us from all directions, including political, economic and technological. Our competitive landscape is always changing. The way we seek, engage and develop diverse talent is critical. We need to actively look for and embrace uncertainties so that we can understand, manage and respond to them. We need to engage those around us to create a collective knowledge and enable fast implementation of resulting plans; we don't have time to do this job poorly. Taking time to make decisions due to bureaucratic processes, or not involving people early enough, leading to slow implementation, is not something anyone can afford.

This book describes the experiences of many great mid- to senior-level leaders who have had to deal with significant challenges in leading change. Each used their own individual perspectives, styles and a variety of tactics to navigate a path to success. You can learn from them what has worked effectively and what hasn't in leading change. This will enable you to make purposeful, planned and thoughtful change which has been shown to be a recipe for success. Leaders who have considered each success factor carefully have seen their goals translate into results.

CASE STUDY – A CLIENT JOURNEY TO SUCCESS

It's 2008. Many businesses are feeling the strain of the recent recession. In a boutique packaging design company in Toronto, a managing director is looking at her latest financial statements. She sees that revenues are dropping as customers are taking longer to make decisions, due to the uncertainty of the business climate. The company is no longer profitable, and it doesn't look like the environment will improve anytime soon.

She raises her head and reflects that her competitors are also struggling, and even showing signs of going out of business. Clearly changes need to be made – but what and how? She thinks she knows some of the answers and decides that whatever changes she makes, they need to be good for both short- and long-term success, so the company can emerge and grow when the economy improves. She realises that the support of her new management team will be important and that they will need to be part of the decision-making process. Shrewdly, she decides to recruit support to help her structure a way to help to make short-term decisions and, importantly, sustain the business long term.

The urgency of the situation and the newness of the team lead to her choosing a simple approach: completing an environmental scan and holding a two-day retreat. This enables the team to make some decisions that are both strategic and insightful. A newly crafted vision combines with actions and commitments to bring the vision to life. The team members identify short-term actions to ensure that the company can sustain its work. Importantly, they integrate these actions into their management team meetings, assigning accountability for completion so that the plan will be implemented.

A year later, the organisation is growing. The work in 2008 has led to a 25% increase in revenue and a move back to profitability during a time when other organisations aren't faring as well. The strategic input of the leadership team has increased as they see and practise the value of thinking of the bigger picture and understanding what's happening in their environment. Staff morale is high, and the previously distant global owner is taking an interest in what is going on in this local operating company.

When the plan is reviewed, there is a marked change in the engagement of the management team. They are able to build on their experience in creating and delivering the plan in the previous year. There is more debate, external awareness and creativity as they develop a plan for the coming year. They gather and use different stakeholder insights to create even more robust plans.

The journey doesn't stop there. The strategic capability of the organisation continues to increase significantly year by year. Each year, the team looks at their plan and refreshes and revitalises their annual goals, seeing how they can grow and sustain their business by creating new insights to inform their approach. This includes:

- Getting first-hand input from customers (and thus strengthening those relationships)
- Engaging their growing number of employees by running focus groups
- Involving their increasingly interested global stakeholders

Over the years, the landscape continues to change. Customers are looking for different offerings, and competitors are moving into either being commodity businesses or exploring a more niche offering. Digital strategies are becoming increasingly relevant, and both customers and competitors are discovering how they can apply these. The business environment is getting more complex, and now the team has the tools to understand what is going on and how they can best position for continued growth.

What they once saw as a stretch in getting stakeholder perspectives as part of their strategic planning, they now see as essential input. This enables the local operating company to be a true partner with its global stakeholders, either by contributing capabilities or by bringing global resources to local clients. Implementation processes are stronger, with clearer accountability and measures for success. The team members each understand their strengths and continue to hone them to deliver success.

The strong planning foundation has stood the company in good stead. Over several years, there have been people and leadership changes, including new managing directors, and each year the team has customised the approach to change depending on the environment and the capability of the team members to respond to the many new complexities. They have been able to understand what is important for their business and to ride the many waves of change.

The management team in this case study was successful in the face of uncertainty for many reasons. They:

- Built the team's strategic capability

- Chose how to change

- Had a facilitator

- Involved people

- Made differences work

- Measured and monitored success

- Met effectively

- Implemented flawlessly

I have seen these success factors in my experiences with many other companies, so I've dedicated a chapter to each one.

I will use case studies and personal stories that illustrate how to use these factors, and each chapter will end with some key takeaways. But before you read about each of the factors of leading change in Chapters 2–9, Chapter 1 defines the role of a change leader and introduces some of the terminology used in leading change.

This book is not a step-by-step methodology to change leadership; instead, it is aimed at sharing collective experiences so that you can benefit from what great leaders have done in making change happen effectively. If you head up an organisation or are responsible for supporting leaders and are struggling with making long-lasting change happen, or you want to lead change from any position in an organisation, this book is for you.

1
The Role Of A Change Leader

This chapter defines the scope of your role as a leader of change and some of the terms that we will use in later chapters to explore the success factors of leading change.

As a leader of change, you (or your team) have to:

- Understand change
- Create and implement strategy
- Involve people in creating strategy
- Use change-management approaches
- Sponsor change projects
- Create a culture and live your values

- Communicate change
- Ensure people have the capability to change
- Recognise and reinforce success
- Influence others

Understand change

CASE STUDY – A GROWING COMPANY MANAGES FOR CHANGE

A medium-size consulting organisation was growing. Its current organisational structure was unwieldy, and the managing director was finding that much of her time was being taken up by her increasing number of direct reports. She recognised that there was a change that needed to be managed.

She created the future state of her organisation by involving each of her current direct reports. They agreed the principles that the organisation was going to follow and what options would work using these principles.

The implementation of this change was successful because:

- The management team was involved in the design of the new structure
- There was a transparent and thoughtful process
- The management team communicated the impact to each of their team members

- Meeting designs that would work for the new structure were part of the new way of working for the organisation, so rollout of the structure was smooth

This enabled the team to create a structure that would sustain the company for the next few years as it doubled in size.

Change can be simply defined as the process of moving between the current state that you are operating in and the future state that you plan to be operating in.[2] To make a change, you need to be clear about these two states and the difference between them. When you create this clarity, the reasons *why* the change is necessary become evident (in the example above, these were growth and the inefficiency of the current structure).

Understanding what is driving the change (what is wrong with the current state) and what is inspiring it (the vision of a better future state) creates a rationale. Clarify what you don't want to change (in the example above, the management team liked the small number of meetings and the close-knit culture they had) so you can retain these in your future state.

The difference between the two states will also inform you about *how* you will make change happen. This is most effective if you can involve people who are directly impacted, as happened in the above example. If this becomes unwieldy due to the size of the organisation, you need to consider other communication mechanisms.

By clearly defining the current state that you are operating in and the future state that you are planning to get to, you will clarify the size and impact of the change. Change is sometimes labelled as 'transactional' or 'transformational' and you can apply different methodologies to manage it. Unfortunately, this is not as easy as just labelling a change and applying a set methodology, as you will need to consider many nuances.

In the example above, the management team used simple tools to ensure that the change was implemented smoothly and rapidly. Choosing the right tools for the job is important and there are many to select from – we will discuss some of these later in this chapter.

Create and implement strategy

Creating and implementing strategy is a critical part of leading change. Effective change leadership needs to start early, ideally as you develop strategy. The skill of **strategic thinking** – the capability to think ahead and across organisational barriers – is important for leaders and their teams.

There are many definitions of what strategy is, and recently business experts have linked the planning aspects of strategy to implementing it.

The strategy process contains three steps:

- Understanding your current environment

- Creating a vision for the future

- Developing and implementing plans to achieve the future vision

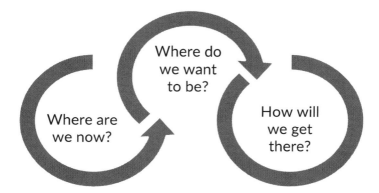

Each of these three elements in creating strategy contains many tools (this is not a comprehensive list):

- Understanding your current environment:

  - External and internal environmental scans like competitive analysis, political, economic, social and technology (PEST) analysis and strength, weaknesses, opportunities and threats (SWOT) analysis[3]

  - Prioritising key issues

- Creating a vision for the future:
  - Vision
  - Value proposition
  - Mission statements
  - Business model generation
  - Objectives, goals, targets, measures, metrics, performance indicators
- Developing and implementing plans to achieve the future vision:
  - Strategies, strategic initiatives, imperatives
  - Action plans, tactics
  - Scorecards, dashboards
  - Accountability

Take a pragmatic approach when you are developing and implanting strategy. Use terminology that your organisation has adopted in the past to avoid introducing another change. If there is no or confusing terminology, then keep it simple and use these terms, which I will use in this book.

Environmental scan – a description of what is happening now outside your organisation that will impact you in the next one to three years, and what you see happening within your organisation now.

This is often encapsulated within a SWOT matrix and ideally boiled down to three to five key issues.

Vision – a description of what your organisation will become in a set timeframe (usually three to five years in rapidly evolving small-to-medium organisations). A vision comprises of three or four sentences that describe the perspective of each group of stakeholders (eg customers, employees, shareholders) on what the organisation will look like. The creation of this vision includes decision making by the leadership of your organisation to narrow in on the specific future that they envisage.

Goals – a description of how you will measure that your organisation has achieved its vision. Goals are set for the same timeline as your vision (three to five years).

Objectives – the intermediate goals that you set to ensure your organisation is tracking towards its long-term goals. Objectives are often set on an annual basis.

Measures – a quantitative description of how your organisation evaluates success.

Targets – the quantitative goal you set for each measure that will show progress.

Stakeholders – the groups of people who are important to your organisation. These groups will include employees, customers, partners, suppliers and funders/investors.

Value proposition/purpose – what your organisation will deliver to specified customers in the more immediate future, including its unique capability to serve.

Strategic initiatives – the three to five big initiatives that will address your organisation's key issues and get you to its vision. Each initiative will have a goal(s) associated with it.

Projects – a coordinated set of activities that move your organisation from its current state to its future state. An initiative can be a project, but not all projects are big enough to be labelled as initiatives.

Action plans – the detailed to-do list within each strategic initiative, with timelines and accountabilities (who will do what).

Involve people in creating strategy

You cannot create strategy in a vacuum. Involving people in developing and implementing strategy means you can attain your desired future effectively.

Developing and implementing strategy

My first project as an external consultant was a fantastic intellectual experience, project managing the development of a supply chain strategy, from the manufacturing of ingredients, through mixing and packaging, and finally to checking out of the product at the grocery store. We built complex models, creating and testing different scenarios to see how we could develop the most effective distribution channels. We filled two binders with the results of the work, but I don't know if it was ever implemented.

Since then, I have had experiences when I have worked with teams who have handed me their strategy and agreed that it would be good if it could be implemented. We've had to do a bit of backtracking to make it work, reengaging with the organisation leaders on why the strategy was developed and clarifying the desired future.

Implementing change involves key stakeholders, whether they are customers, employees, or other departments. The more you involve people in understanding their environment and creating a vision, the more engaged and motivated they will be when it is time to implement the strategy.

The value of involvement

Having been both an external and internal consultant for nearly fifteen years, I was appointed to my first people-management role. It was an exciting time as I had the opportunity to create a new department that could really contribute to the effectiveness of an entire division in both managing risk and saving money. My great team were experts in their fields and not afraid to voice their concerns. I was excited to share my vision with them and help them to define how they could contribute.

We set goals for the year and off we set on our journey.

Despite some start-up challenges, we made progress and I thought it would be a good idea to pause, reflect and celebrate our early success, as well as ensuring we were on track to achieve our goals. All great work for a new leader, or so I thought.

Luckily, I also had the presence of mind to ask the team what they would like to cover if we did take time to reflect, and one person said, 'Could we discuss why the department was set up, please?' A lightbulb moment (or blinding spotlight for me). This brought home to me the importance of individuals not just being told (or maybe not even being told) why change is happening, but truly understanding and integrating the bigger picture and rationale so that they feel involved and can focus on the what and how to achieve the change. By the end of the session where I facilitated what the team saw as key drivers for change, their motivation had changed. It marked a distinct improvement in the way the team worked together – not just completing their tasks, but focusing on what needed to be done to achieve the organisation's goals.

An even more powerful exercise was when we clarified our own personal purposes and linked them to departmental and organisational goals. That both built team cohesion and inspired individuals to follow their own purpose.

Simon Sinek suggests that many businesses know *what* they do and *how* they do it, but few know *why*.[4] Great strategic thinking starts with clarifying organisational purpose. A critical part of inspiring and bringing employees on the journey to implement strategic thinking is to jointly identify organisational purpose and enable people to link it with their own personal purpose. In any change that your organisation is considering, it's important to describe the why or the purpose of the change.

You can just *tell* people how to change, but you will achieve an increasing level of commitment when you *sell* to them why it is important. And this commitment increases the more you *involve* them in the process. If you create something together, then your team members will feel they have a real stake in its success.

Intuitively, this makes sense, but sometimes leaders of change take what they see as a shorter route. They define a future without input, thinking that is their job, and simply tell people what they need to do. But people need time to buy into the future state before they implement it. This typically takes longer than involving them at the start, and it is not as motivating.

Strategy is about both creating and implementing the future direction of your organisation. Creation with other stakeholders enables stronger implementation. There are links between strategy and change, and you'll need similar capabilities when you're implementing strategic initiatives or change projects.

In leading change, you need to determine what changes need to be made and use a portfolio approach. Relate each change to the future state your organisation wants to achieve so everyone can see the link.

Use change-management approaches

Change management can be defined as the collective term for the different approaches to preparing, support-ing and helping individuals, teams and organisations to bring about organisational change. There are some great management methodologies that can enable change to happen. Whether it is Prosci's ADKAR,[5] Kotter's eight-step process,[6] or the Change Manage-ment Institute certification process,[7] each methodology brings its own set of valuable tools and approaches.

CASE STUDY – AUTOMATION

A global manufacturer was about to implement a new system for automating the way it manufactured product. It would change the way the teams worked: instead of them making manual notes, all of the information would be automatically recorded.

The manufacturer had gone through a lot of other organisational change before this one. The management team decided it would be useful to apply a strong change-management methodology to the situation. Some of the elements that were particularly useful were:

- Assessing the successes and failures of previous changes. This enabled them to continue successful approaches (eg managers reinforcing the importance of the change) and apply what they had learned (eg timing of the communications and not using methodology, which had previously slowed down the process, for the sake of it).

- Understanding the groups that would be impacted by the change. This enabled the management team to clarify their roles (eg making the change, supporting the change, removing barriers, reinforcing).

- Reinforcing the change by consciously thinking about the links to performance. This enabled the change to be embedded in people's day-to-day jobs as they were recognised for their shift in behaviours.

- Spending time on clarifying how success would be measured. The direct link to quality of the product and the resulting financial impact was important to continue to focus leadership attention.

This strong methodology allowed for a smooth transition to automation.

You have to select change-management tools carefully as they can be seen as bureaucratic and slowing down the process. This will happen if you religiously follow a methodology with no flexibility. As a leader of change, you need to guide the process by selecting the tools and approach that are right for your situation and not using unnecessary tools that can slow down implementation. More about this in Chapter 3.

Change leadership involves not just change-management methodologies, but the proactive determination of what changes need to be made. It encompasses the development of strategy as this is where change should start. Most importantly, change leadership implies that leaders have a critical role implementing strategy to ensure changes contribute to achieving an organisation's vision. This implementation role is described more in Chapter 9.

Sponsor change projects

Time and again, studies to assess why change fails find the sponsorship of change by leaders is a key factor.[8] *Sponsorship* is the role that a leader takes in a specific strategic initiative to support a *project manager* who is responsible for coordinating the delivery of an action plan. Sponsors coach project managers and remove barriers to progress.

When you are a great sponsor, you are motivated and aligned with bigger organisational priorities (strategic initiatives). This enables you to make appropriate decisions about resources and timelines. What can happen is sponsors think that when they have defined a vision for a project and put appropriate resources in place to communicate and train those impacted, their job is done.

Another common pitfall can be the sponsor's desire to jump into a project manager role. They feel that if a project is not happening fast enough, all it needs is better project management. Rather than coaching the project manager and understanding how they can remove barriers to progress, the sponsor starts to micromanage.

It's change sponsorship that really counts, ie how you act, behave and reinforce the change you want to see. Your willingness as a sponsor to take risks by delegating authority, and then supporting the project manager or team if failures occur, is critical to successful change.

There is, however, more to leading change than sponsoring specific projects or initiatives.

Create a culture and live your values

The definition of **culture** as 'the way we do things around here' is strongly influenced by leaders. Leaders' behaviours shape culture. The culture of an organisation will shape how quickly the organisation can adapt to changing circumstances, how it can bounce back from adverse environmental changes and how willing it is to take risks. In short, your leadership behaviour can create an environment where change can thrive.

You can embody your culture by defining **values** as 'the principles that help you make decisions'.[9] The importance of creating values is to share expectations of how your company will achieve its vision, but even more importantly, as a leader, you have to live those values through the decisions and actions you take every day.

CASE STUDY – CULTURE AS AN ANCHOR

One organisation was going through a series of mergers and acquisitions and could see much change on its horizon. The leadership team identified what had served them well in the past and described the performance culture that they were currently working in. They thought about their potential future and decided that no matter what organisation they were going to be working in, elements of their current performance-based culture would be valuable.

The team members were able to use their description of culture as an anchor to engage people in a newly acquired organisation. This provided a solid foundation for growth as the merger process unfolded.

The more you can give people a sense of what will not change, a backbone or infrastructure that they can rely on, the more flexible and creative you will enable them to be in the areas where you need them to be innovative. McKinsey uses an analogy of a phone which has a stable hardware and operating system, as well as the flexible apps that can be changed to create agility.[10] Holding this tension in the organisation allows you to get the best of both worlds.

If you are true to the vision and values you set (which will rarely change), modify your strategic initiatives as necessary (which will sometimes change) and pivot on the actions you need to take (which will often change). This will allow you to adapt and change quickly without confusion to employees and other stakeholders. It will also build a strong culture that enables you to succeed.

Sometimes change is so overwhelming, it's hard to remember that some familiar things will stay the same. It's good to acknowledge this so you can ground yourself and the organisation.

Communicate change

Communication is a critical part of leading change, but it is not all that you need. Too often, leadership teams build communication plans around sending messages out via various creative channels, but do not prepare themselves to take their role as leaders for change to be successful.

We've all likely been involved with change communication, either as leaders who have had to talk to teams or departments, or as recipients hearing news that will impact us. In any change scenario, there can be a mixture of positive and negative consequences, depending on individuals' situations. What you think is good news may be perceived by others as bad news, and vice versa.

People often see change as negative, especially if they feel it is being 'done' to them. As you learn to be a better leader of change, you need to harness your emotional intelligence and empathy skills to continue your journey of becoming more adaptable in the face of change.

Communication plays an important part in leading change, and having a plan is critical. The detail and foresight you need depends on the size of the change, the impact it will have and your skills in navigating through a world of multiple challenges. You will find tips on how you can do this effectively in Chapter 9.

Ensure people have the capability to change

Training, like communication, can be seen as a panacea to successful change. If you show people how to do something and give them the skills and tools to do it, then change will happen. Of course, this misses out essential elements: people must want to change and feel like they are in an environment that will enable that change.

Training is important, and a leader's role in making change happen is to understand what training people need. Do they have the **capability** – a combination of the skills, knowledge and experience – to make the change you're asking of them? Do they require classroom/online training or a place to practise their skills? Is it already within their capabilities to adopt the change? Do they need a coach or a helpline, written guidelines or a checklist?

It's important that you ensure the timing of the training comes at a point when people are able to apply the knowledge they have gained. In the case study 'Automation', one of the leadership team's learnings prior to the implementation of the new system was that previously, training had been done too early. This was frustrating for all involved as people tended to forget what they had learned before they were able to apply it.

Training can be a necessary part of change as people must know what is expected of them, but this needs to be integrated into a wider plan.

Recognise and reinforce success

As a change leader, you need to recognise those who have changed and reinforce their new behaviour. If you are their line manager, you will likely have figured out whether people respond better to formal or informal recognition. It could take the form of a new developmental opportunity, public acknowledgements or private thank yous; it is not always about a pay rise.

Your role as leader is to employ what works for your people with other change leaders to ensure fairness. In change programmes, recognise team successes as well as (or instead of) individual successes, especially when future states depend on more collaboration and teamwork.

It's also critical that you take time to recognise and celebrate milestones achieved. This allows you to reflect and reenergise the team, as well as building the momentum for continued change. If the change is critical, then building adoption of a new way of working into performance objectives is a strong way for you to reinforce the change.

As you start your journey as a leader of change, remember to plan how you'll recognise that change. Take the time now to build a climate that reinforces the successes that the organisation's teams have achieved in the past. Recognise behaviours that demonstrate movement into the future state, tailor recognition to what people appreciate – it's not just about money – and take time to celebrate success.

Influence others

Influencing others is a critical skill in change leadership. Often as a change leader, you have to influence your peers or others over whom you don't have organisational power. When you are part of a cohesive and aligned leadership team, this is easy.

Sometimes you need to move outside your organisational boundaries and influence others to do something different. Building trust before you need to make a change is important, so making connections and understanding their perspective is a great first step. Consider who will be impacted by the change you are leading. Take every opportunity to build trust before you need to lead a change by connecting with other people.

Key takeaways

- Change is the process of moving between the current and future state. Define these two states to enable the *why* and *how* of the change your organisation needs to be clear.

- Strategy is understanding your current environment, creating a direction for the future and implementing plans to achieve that future.

- Use simple and consistent terminology to help you lead change effectively.

- Involve people in developing strategy to enable motivation and alignment.

- Link all changes to your strategic direction.

- Select change-management approaches thoughtfully.

- Be a great change sponsor who coaches project managers and removes barriers to progress. Don't be a 'super project manager'.

- Match what you say with how you act and create a culture that enables change. Culture is shaped by leaders' everyday behaviour.

- Acknowledge what will stay the same.

- Have a communication plan in the context of a broader change plan.

- Give people the skills they need to make change happen.

- Create a plan to recognise behaviours that demonstrate movement into the future state. Tailor your recognition to suit individuals.

- Make connections and build trust before you need it.

2
Build Strategic Capability

This is the first success factor of the eight I listed in the Introduction. It's an important factor because, particularly as leaders, you need to think strategically (ie have the capability to think ahead and across organisational barriers).

I used to think it was only the top leaders of organisations who needed to be strategic. But wouldn't it be amazing if everyone in your organisation and your partners (customers, suppliers) were strategic thinkers? If they were, you would see organisations:

- Adapt to changing circumstances readily

- Working seamlessly across functions and with partner organisations

- Whose employees are engaged and aligned

- Whose talent is consistently developing, creating the leaders of the future

- That produce results year after year

In short, organisations that are successful for the long term.

This chapter will describe what happens when different stakeholders think more strategically. Through case studies, you will see how a combination of strategic thinking and actively planning for the future can not only build capability, but also lead to tangible results.

Think before acting

A key part of strategic thinking is the importance of considering long-term and broader impacts before acting. In the frenetic pace of the world we live in, we're encountering an increasing pressure to do rather than think. Being agile implies moving quickly. Articles abound that tell us to stop procrastinating and just do it.

But there is a real danger to just doing something – anything – that gives the impression that you are action oriented and moving things forward. This is especially true if you are leading an organisation. If you are a leader who doesn't think before acting, then this will be reflected throughout the rest of the organisation, and you will end up with chaos rather than agility.

The value of the pause button

Recently, I had the pleasure of working with someone whose team said he was a superb leader. I asked the team members why they thought that, and they said, 'He stops us and makes us think' and 'He presses the pause button so we can check we are heading in the right direction'.

I learned pretty quickly in my interactions with this leader that this was true, but it never felt like anything was being slowed down. Instead, the team had increased confidence that the project was moving in the right direction. By taking the time to name and remove barriers to progress, he ensured goals were reached more quickly and smoothly.

How do you know *when* to think before acting? Here are some examples:

- Think if what you are doing will impact the long-term future of the organisation. It is your job as a leader (at all levels) to consider this and choose the most effective option.

- Think whether what you are doing is the highest priority for the organisation. Sometimes the most urgent things have to be dealt with first, but this is not always true – is it?

- Think especially when there is a lot of pressure to do something. It may seem counterintuitive, but pressing the pause button could identify a more effective way of achieving your goals.

- Think if you have delegated an activity to someone else and they are not doing what you think they should be. How can you support them without jumping in and doing the task yourself or micromanaging?

- Think if there is a better way of getting to a destination by involving more people in the decision making.

Don't procrastinate but take the time to think through the consequences of your decisions clearly. There will be times when you need to take decisive action, but you still need to think before you act. It's too easy to slip into action first and suffer chaotic consequences as a result of a drive to busyness.

Empower your frontline teams

CASE STUDY – FROM SERVICE PROVIDER TO PARTNER

An internal operations team within a growing biotech company needed to shift from being service providers who simply gave transactional support, to becoming business partners and change leaders who proposed direction and led the implementation of that direction. The team members had talked to their internal customers and leadership team, who had fed back that they valued the strong technical expertise the team brought. Now the time was right to add to their role by bringing insights into the decision making that would enable profitable growth.

They constructed a proposition which described how they planned to add value to their internal customer in the future and integrated how to achieve this into their annual objectives, along with defining their contribution to their broader organisational plan. This resulted in an aligned department that was excited about the value they could bring, along with the tangible plans for how to get there. The team members also had a clearer understanding of their individual functional roles and how they could support each other on a day-to-day basis. The department continued to move along the spectrum from being a supplier of information to being regarded as a strategic partner.

This group improved their strategic thinking skills by:

- Talking to their cross-functional colleagues and understanding what would be valuable

- Playing a more important and insightful role by participating in company annual planning

- Planning their own future and reviewing and adapting annually

A great way to grow your skills is to watch experts do the work, then work alongside them, and finally take on the task yourself with an expert there in case you need to ask questions. Having the opportunity to watch others and get their support gives you the confidence to do a task by yourself, both as an individual and an organisation. The group in our case study did this by watching a facilitator and their leader engaging them through a structured process.

It is important for frontline teams to think strategically. By thinking across functions and on a long-term horizon, your teams will build the capabilities they need for the future. This level of thinking will empower them to:

- Bring their unique perspectives to the overall direction of the organisation by feeding into the decision-making process

- Challenge existing directions based on their frontline insights

- Implement strategic direction effectively due to their increased understanding of the bigger picture

Lead your department strategically

CASE STUDY – STRENGTHENING PERFORMANCE VIA SHARED GOALS

A new global team had been put in place to coordinate and oversee the activities of individual country functions, and a new vice president had been appointed to bring cohesion to the team. The team had clear business deliverables and individual objectives, but little sense of shared accountability. An opportunity existed to strengthen performance by sharing common goals and having a long-term vision of success.

The team developed shared annual objectives by identifying common issues and focusing on what was important for success. Then they articulated the behaviours for success in achieving objectives. The implementation director identified and implemented tracking mechanisms so they achieved the annual goals.

The following year, the team developed a long-term vision for success and created a one-year plan to move towards the vision. The tracking mechanisms were simplified and success behaviours clarified. This resulted in stronger teamwork between individuals, more effective meetings and an increased capability to achieve goals.

Setting annual goals for an organisation can be challenging, especially when you work in an environment that is constantly changing, but taking time to reflect, connect with colleagues and look forward can be invaluable in reenergising and focusing your team on the year ahead. If everyone is working towards the same end goal, it is much more likely you will have a successful year.

This can be the first step to more strategic long-term thinking, and is sometimes easier to do than jumping into a long-term broad-thinking planning exercise. Once you and others have gone through this process together as a team, department or organisation, you will all be more prepared to take a strategic view, leading to long-term sustainability. It is more practical than having to keep developing a full-scale strategic plan.

Here are some simple steps to take:

- Understand where you are today and celebrate your successes:
  - What have you achieved over the last twelve months? If you have moved from once-a-year individual reviews to ongoing performance feedback, it's even more important to take time to reflect on overall team achievements.
  - What is going on with your customers and stakeholders that may impact what you can achieve in the upcoming year?
  - What is outstanding from the past year that you need to carry forward?
- Identify how you will measure success in the coming year (and beyond):
  - How did you know you were successful last year?
  - What will success look like from a financial perspective?
  - How will your customers and partners see success?
  - What internal measures are important?
  - Imagine you are looking back at the year in a year's time and create a picture of what has to be done to get there.

- Do a reality check:

  - What are the big projects/activities that will need to happen?

  - Who will take on ownership for each of those projects?

  - Do you have the resources (budget and people) to get to where you want to be?

  - What would stop you achieving these goals and how will you address this?

  - Do you need to modify targets or timelines to make goals achievable?

- Agree how you will need to behave as a team to get these results:

  - When will you meet to review progress? Consider more frequent, faster and informal feedback loops.

  - How will you and your teams support each other?

  - How will you hold each other accountable?

- Communicate your goals:

  - Who else needs to know about your goals? Customers? Partners? Suppliers? Peers?

  - How will you engage them so you can achieve your annual goals?

Learning is not a one-stop deal, so it doesn't have to be done all at once. A step-by-step process increasing your time horizon and the breadth of your thinking as an organisation keeps an appropriate balance between planning and doing. By taking these steps as a departmental or team leader, you can be pragmatic and move forward as well as growing your ability to think strategically.

Lead your growing organisation thoughtfully

There are some special challenges when organisations start growing bigger. As a leader of change, you need to be purposeful and intentional about that change. There is an inflection point at which a business realises it needs hierarchy and structure as a solid backbone for future success, otherwise processes are reinvented anew every time a product is launched or a new resource hired.

In some cases, there are no processes. With limited resources in a growing company, this cannot continue, as you'll use more resources and time creating processes than following a well-established and efficient one. Additionally, and perhaps more concerning if you are a founder or entrepreneur, there is a possibly justified fear of losing your innovative and agile culture if you see too much process equating to bureaucracy. But how much process is too much?

It depends on the specific organisation and the environment it works in. Here are three tips for getting that balance between agility and efficiency right:

- Be explicit about values and behaviours. As a leadership team, discuss, agree and write down the values you want to see in your growing organisation and how you will model the behaviours that exemplify these values. There is a connection between ways of working and the processes you adopt, but you can design behaviours by defining and reinforcing those that are important to continued success.

- Design processes to be minimalist. Don't adopt them directly from larger organisations without looking to reduce or abandon steps that are not adding value. Many growing organisations look to larger organisations for the expertise that they have undoubtedly acquired over many years, but unfortunately history has a way of building in redundancies which don't add value in new situations. Always ask the question, 'What is the purpose of this process?' and only have steps in your process that directly fulfil this purpose.

- Review your processes regularly and actively for their fitness. Make it part of the leaders' jobs to look for ways to abandon activities.

By applying these three tips, you can actively create the organisation you are growing into rather than allowing the organisation to become unwieldy and bureaucratic. It is strategic thinking at its best. Take the time to consider your long-term future, so when there is pressure to act immediately, you will be able to apply this thinking. Not only will you see business results, you will also build the foundation for a sustainable organisation with a strong strategic-thinking capability.

Use planning to build capabilities

CASE STUDY – AN EFFECTIVE AND SUSTAINABLE PROCESS

A 500-person organisation had a complex planning process that used many tools. Reorganisations had led to confusion about handoffs between different departments. Changes and initiatives never seemed to stick. Innovation and new ways of doing things were not valued.

The management team assessed existing processes and tools, and gathered information via one-on-ones and functional focus groups to identify strengths, weaknesses and priorities for change.

A solutions workshop for the leadership team identified changes to the process. As this process evolved, the newly appointed planning manager got more involved, moving from being an observer and co-designing workshops to leading the process of implementing change and working with sponsors for success. This resulted in a leadership team that was engaged in the new process and committed to maintaining ongoing focus.

Results a year later showed an increase or maintenance in each performance dimension of the planning process, with 35–60% increases for the dimensions of accountability and having a well-defined process. The organisation had a sustainable process, the planning manager's capabilities in change management increased and the organisation itself grew its strategic thinking capability.

There were many reasons why this organisation grew its capability to think strategically:

- A clear process enabled everyone to understand what was expected from them.

- The planning manager took accountability for collecting insights, which enabled her to challenge the content of the leadership team plan.

- Leadership planning meetings were focused on cross-functional decision making rather than sharing information.

- Transfer of decision making from the CEO to the leadership team resulted in richer strategic insights.

Planning by doing enables you to gain an immediate impact from your activity as well as building capability for the future.

Partner with your suppliers

Organisations are relying more and more on various kinds of partnerships to grow, streamline their operations and enter new markets. These partnerships can be in the form of joint ventures, strategic alliances, or simple preferred supplier-customer transactions.

There are several reasons why organisations are partnering:

- Small businesses can hit an inflection point where the need to scale up quickly becomes paramount. Reassess all your resources and determine what is really needed from a bottom-up/zero base. This may mean dropping/eliminating some resources or reallocating versus adding. If additional resources are core to business success, there are two options. The first is to grow by hiring and training resources, but an alternative is to partner with organisations whose focus is on the expertise you are seeking and contract out to them.

- Contracting out research activities that need specialised expertise is becoming more popular when an organisation is seeing its core expertise in development or commercialisation. High-volume efficient processes are also being contracted out with resultant success for both partners as they realise efficiencies and innovations.

- The increased complexity of doing business. Opportunities for growth are endless – new geographies, new technologies and products are in abundance. The challenge is taking advantage of these opportunities, and often to do this, you need specialised capabilities which would be expensive to build and not cost effective to have in house. Examining what is critical for you to have in your business vs what can be outsourced is a smart strategy. For example, do you need to invest in expensive manufacturing facilities if you can outsource to an experienced manufacturer?

- Accessing top talent. If you are a small business, then hiring the best people on a full-time basis does not always make sense. For example, a small business cannot hire the strategic human resources (HR) advice that may make all the difference as its workforce starts to grow. Accessing HR expertise through outsourcing can be a great strategy until you can justify having an in-house resource.

- Expanding into new markets. If you are considering moving into a different geography, then partnering with experts in local markets can help you. They can advise you on working with regulatory authorities, different legal processes or understanding various marketing channels. This can save much frustration.

- By combining the expertise of different companies, you can deliver more than you could achieve alone. For example, as a consultant, if I partner with project managers, communication experts and strategy analysts, I can offer a broader range of services to customers. This means customers need only build a relationship with one partner. Some customers like to have this 'one-stop' service.

Although there are many reasons why partnerships are becoming more common, all too often, scant attention is paid to making these partnerships the best they can be, with legal contracts and service-level agreements tending to be the only bases for successfully working together. These are important foundations to any partnership between organisations, but not the only ingredient for success.

Why don't more organisations take on partners? Trust is one of the biggest issues. You need to:

- Work through various challenges such as how intellectual property (IP) will be owned

- Identify which processes and governance you and your partner(s) will use

- Agree talent-sharing policies before you start partnerships

- Have contracts and service-level agreements

The opportunity is to take partnership to a more strategic level where you agree to cooperate to advance your *mutual* interests in the short and long term and gain a competitive advantage in your marketplace. If you can agree joint long-term goals and partnership principles, you will have an immediate benefit in increasing the strength of the relationship. As you take the time to understand more about your partners' perspectives, you will also grow your capability to think strategically. This will be a foundation to create a mutually beneficial and synergistic partnership that is sustainable for the long term.

There's more about how you can achieve this in Chapter 6.

Key takeaways

- Think strategically to create an organisation that is successful for the long term.

- Take time to think before you act.

- Encourage everyone to be strategic. Frontline teams can add many insights and grow their capabilities to be ready for the future. Departments will ensure that they are thinking cross-functionally and add value for the long term.

- Take the time to plan when you are growing so that you can build success that is sustainable.

- You can build your strategic thinking capability step by step. Take the time to think cross functionally for the short term as a first step.

- Grow your strategic capability by doing and use others to guide you to achieve business results.

- Be strategic with partnerships to have a long-term payoff with an immediate short-term improvement in relationships.

3
Choose How To Change

The second important success factor of leading for change is choosing how to change. If you choose wisely, change can be empowering, simple and focused. If you don't choose your approach or make ineffective choices, change can feel overwhelming, uncontrolled and ineffective.

Make change empowering, not overwhelming

The hare or the tortoise approach

One of my tasks as a product development manager was to liaise with suppliers to specify what my teams needed from them to ensure our products would work during the manufacturing process and for the end user. The product I was developing was innovative and we were learning what the technical specification needed to be for individual components.

Two suppliers were working with me. One was incredibly accommodating, and if I asked for a change, they immediately acted on it. Unfortunately, the consequences of their rapid action led to many shortcuts, which resulted in the component failing.

The second supplier needed me to provide more evidence to prove that it was worth them making a change. This was harder for me (and my company) to accept at first, but their approach got to a workable solution faster. They provided different samples and varied each aspect in a controlled fashion, compared to the first supplier who took my ideas and sprinted with them.

There are several factors at play dictating whether change will be overwhelming or empowering, such as your individual propensity to change, how much you are/have been in control of the change, and the degree to which the change will affect you personally. Ask yourself what your first reaction is when changes occur at work. Are you one of the first to jump onboard, or do you need time to think and evaluate pros and cons before deciding to change?

How to love change

When I became aware of how much I love change at work, it was enlightening to understand that others around me did not share that same desire. I had just taken on leading a new team, many of whom valued the past and the expertise they had grown in managing current processes. I realised how important it was to listen to them so we could properly explore the impact of the change before implementing it. I learned to step back and understand how they were feeling.

We explored advantages and disadvantages of the change together so we could reduce the sense of being overwhelmed and increase the feelings of being in control. It helped us to balance the speed of change and manage the risks we were taking.

In both of these personal stories, it was important for me to involve and consider the point of view of others impacted by the change. By listening to concerns and adapting a solution that integrates others' suggestions, you can obtain a better result and implement change more smoothly.

Choose when to plan

Reflecting with your team will enable you to share what you are observing and decide if it impacts your direction. There are some key triggers that can alert you to the fact it is time to reflect and plan:

- The external environment is changing quickly. Whether it is political uncertainty, customer or consumer demands, disruptive technology or new competitors, more and more, you are simply responding to what is going on in the external environment. While it is good to be responsive, if you don't do this in a thoughtful manner with your organisation aligning, it can cause misunderstanding, chaos and confusion, leading to less than optimum performance. External changes will also lead to a need to reassess your initiatives and projects to evaluate whether the risks and benefits have changed and if you have the resources to continue with them.

- The organisation has been growing rapidly. It is chaotic and processes do not exist or are being reinvented. It's time to introduce some structure, but not so much that it becomes overwhelming. Taking time to be thoughtful about this will help you achieve the right balance.

- Specialists are being promoted into managers or additional management layers are being added. As this happens, there is a tendency for silos and functional thinking to take over rather than the cross-functional interactions you need for success.

- There are conflicting priorities and resource needs. You are acting as a referee between your team members on a frequent basis, which suggests it's not clear what the overall priorities for the organisation are.

- Your business model is changing. Whether it's from a single product to a multiproduct line, or how you will outsource or partner with others, or growing from a development organisation to a commercial organisation, or mergers/acquisitions are changing what your organisation looks like, there are many factors that can lead to thoughtful consideration of what your ideal business model should be.

- You are the change, ie you are in a new leadership role. After a few months of being in this new role, you have sized up the organisation and think you know what changes need to be made. This is a great time to get team input, validate your thoughts and ensure everyone is on the same page.

If you find yourself in one or more of these situations, it is time to stop, reflect and realign together with your team. Consider *what* you have observed; ask 'So what' (does that mean?) and 'Now what' (will you do as a result?).[11] As an organisation, consider a strategic planning process so you can engage with your team and broader stakeholders.

Select your planning approach

CASE STUDY - THE VALUE OF A PLANNING STRUCTURE

A small luxury-goods company had many day-to-day issues it wanted to act on as a matter of urgency. No one seemed to take accountability for actions or discuss expectations. This concentrated too much work with a few senior people and frustrated some middle managers because of the bottleneck that had been created. There was never time to sit down and reflect on what needed to happen, and thinking longer term than a few weeks was hard as the day-to-day needs of various seasonal activities arose.

By taking a few hours every couple of months or so, the management team created a planning structure that worked for them. It meant they could identify issues and agree actions. By setting up a tracking mechanism, they ensured accountability became more visible and their capability to plan grew. This enabled them to be in control of their process.

Some people hate to plan, believing it restricts their flexibility to respond and arguing they work in such a changeable environment that it's simply not worth it. Maybe they've experienced a turgid bureaucratic process that was only focused on financials, over time growing into a chore to endure every year. Other people actively love planning. They enjoy thinking about the future rather than working on achieving reality.

The sweet spot is to have a vision *and* a plan of action that results in you achieving your vision. It's important to choose a planning process that works for your organisation so that the time you spend really does add value in delivering results. One size does *not* fit all, so how do you decide what planning process to adopt?

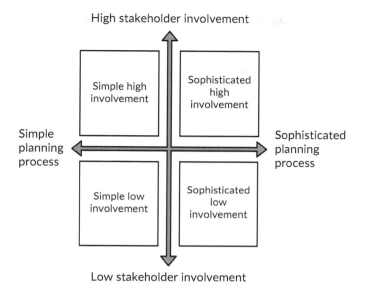

Your planning maturity and capability

If you have never created a long-term plan before, then it's much better to do something simple with a few key people than to create a sophisticated process, using many different planning tools and involving all stakeholders. You don't want a lengthy, overwhelming and impractical process. You can build your level of sophistication gradually to match your capability to think strategically and, more importantly, to implement your plan. This matrix shows options that you can choose to plan effectively, depending on your size and maturity as an organisation.

Current process effectiveness

If you have a planning process already, evaluate what is working so you can improve rather than start from scratch. One organisation's team measured the effectiveness of their planning against a benchmark of good planning and used that to implement a more effective way of doing things. Each year, they improved their process to suit their needs.

Size and complexity of organisation

Smaller organisations rarely need as sophisticated a planning process as larger ones. A good strategic planning process includes key stakeholders right from the start, so when new directions emerge, there is already buy-in, speeding up the adoption of change. Generally larger organisations have more stakeholders, but the increasing diversity of organisations that partner for success can lead to complex small organisations. In these virtual organisations, working to involve partners in your planning can be crucial (see Chapters 2 and 6 for more on partnering).

Speed of environmental changes

If your external environment is changing quickly, then you need to synchronise your planning. If planning takes too long, then external perspectives may be out of date before you action. Conversely, a short planning cycle means you are expending unnecessary effort if your environment hasn't changed. Choose the cadence of your planning cycle deliberately.

Degree of engagement from stakeholders

How critical is it that you engage your stakeholders? It may be important to have partners, employees or shareholders on board with your plans early in your planning cycle, but this needs to be balanced with the upfront time this will take and the need to progress quickly as a result of being clear on your strategic context. Late engagement will delay implementation as stakeholders need time to buy into and adapt to new directions.

Actively decide how to plan by considering your existing capability, the desired degree of stakeholder involvement and your environment.

Create focus and alignment

Remember the days when life was simple? The environment was comparatively static, we as leaders had an idea and we could command our organisation to follow it. There was an automatic alignment of resources.

Command and control organisations are harder to find now. People are part of organisations because they are looking for purpose and want their individual goals to be seen in overall organisational directions.

CASE STUDY – REASSESSING VALUE

The R&D department leaders in a medical device company recognised they needed to reassess their value. Many changes in personnel had occurred in this function and a new leader had been appointed. External drivers had accelerated the organisation's need to have a strong presence with its customers. The sales and marketing team was looking to the medical team for increased value. Employees were strong players within their roles, but little cross-functional understanding existed.

The commercial teams and the medical team provided information about the environment which was shared back so the medical team could identify key issues and construct a value proposition together with success measures. They developed action and communications plans along with tracking mechanisms. The medical function leadership team then became clearer about their value proposition and had practical actions to move them towards realising their value.

In some organisations, leaders assume that people already know what direction they need to go in, but in less mature organisations or ones where there has been significant change internally or externally, this is often not true. Everyone needs to be crystal clear about their current and future purpose, otherwise chaos can ensue. Assumptions are made about why the organisation exists and what an individual's role is within that organisation. Sometimes, these are based on a history that is not the same as today's reality. Without a clear organisational direction, drift is a natural behaviour. Why would anyone move purposefully without a clear direction?

Larger organisations succeed when they inspire their employees at all levels with a powerful vision and clear purpose that is cascaded into strategies and objectives owned by leaders throughout the organisation. Top-down direction is translated to bottom-up deliverables through feedback loops and many different communication mechanisms. This can work extremely well in many cases, but the dark side can be a culture of bureaucracy and red tape that arrives with a resultant lack of agility and innovation. Balancing these opposing forces is only achieved by design, and it's critical for long-term success.

This is not just an issue for large business; it is a critical issue as organisations grow. As we discussed in Chapter 2, there is an inflection point at which a business realises that it has to build in some hierarchy and structure, for example, appointing managers to cascade messages and engage employees. If there is no hierarchy and structure, entrepreneurs spread themselves too thinly and have no time for the strategic work that's necessary to sustain the business.

Sometimes, entrepreneurial founders are resistant to taking a step towards more structure. They want to keep an agile culture and be in touch with their frontline employees, knowing that they can correct any misalignment and redirect the organisation quickly, but there is a point at which this becomes unsustainable and they have to implement new ways of working.

Alignment with partners outside your organisation can be even more difficult than building structure within. If partnerships are important for your success, you will need to create a way of working that is aligned. It won't only be about delivering to contractual requirements, but will include a common vision of success, a shared purpose, and agreements to work jointly towards common goals.

Whatever kind of organisation you are involved with, you need to focus resources on the end goal. Misalignment (whether within or across organisations) is the biggest cause of organisation failure. Spending time resolving issues due to people moving in different directions is a waste of effort. You can't afford this in resource-constrained organisations in today's competitive environment.

These are the steps you can take to realign:

- Ensure all stakeholders understand and internalise *why* the organisation is heading in a specific direction. What is in the external environment that has created the opportunity? What strengths does the organisation have that allow it to respond?

- Co-create an inspiring vision with your key stakeholders (*what*).

- Identify the three to five strategic imperatives (priorities) that you all must address to move towards the vision *(how)*.

- Align stakeholders by agreeing roles, responsibilities *(who)* and timings *(when)* for all priority actions needed to achieve the vision.

- Create mechanisms for monitoring, recognising success and taking actions to ensure ongoing focus.

Although these steps may seem simple, it is not always easy to follow them. Often organisations fail as they find it difficult to prioritise, don't align effectively and rarely have the culture that supports monitoring, but I have seen dramatic results when organisations do follow these steps.

When employees are working on the right priorities, inspired by their purpose as an individual and can see alignment to bigger organisational purpose, it results in organisations delivering their goals. Improve focus and alignment by working with your team to understand the environment and plan how you can add the most value to your stakeholders.

Create autonomy

Creating choices in change

One of my early career memories of change 'being done to me' was when a colleague of mine walked over to my desk and placed a document in front of me that described a new way of working. It was my job described in the document, but I'd had no say in what went into it.

I looked up at her in surprise, and she said, 'This is what you have to do – effective immediately.' Many thoughts went through my mind: first disbelief, then anger. I was to learn later that there is a change curve[12] people use to understand the stages we go through when faced with change, but at the time, I didn't know about that; I just knew that things weren't the way they should be. What was especially difficult was that there seemed no room for me to input or negotiate. I had no say and felt out of control.

A more well-handled change occurred when I was told to move to a satellite office away from the main centre of operations. This time, although I had no say in the decision for my move, I was openly invited to make it work. I could have a hotelling space in the main office, work from home occasionally, have my pick of available offices in the new satellite building if I decided quickly, choose the furniture I wanted etc. I got on board with little hesitation.

This personal story speaks of the importance of *having choices* during change. Maybe you can't create the *what* of change, but you can control or input into the *how*. The ability to clearly define boundaries that are non-negotiable, but allow a space for people to choose what can go within them, is an important change leadership skill, and one to think through before imposing change. It is a disadvantage if you have all the answers as a change leader.

A change leader cannot just focus on big-picture thinking. The skill of 'helicoptering', ie being able to drill down and understand detail, is also important so you can set boundaries, and then listen to and alleviate concerns. Think about ways you will create autonomy and choice by considering what is negotiable in a change and what is not.

Create simplicity

CASE STUDY – INVOLVEMENT AND SIMPLICITY EQUALS CLARITY

A division had to make many changes to the way it operated due to a transitioning external environment and internal corporate direction. A new leader and leadership team had been appointed to navigate this change, and other divisions had expectations of how this division would perform. As a result, employees within the division were uncertain about their roles and their interactions with others.

The leadership team reviewed information from many stakeholders: the executive team, the divisional leadership team, managers and employees. This allowed them to construct a simple value proposition and identify key issues and strategies. The extended leadership team then developed action plans and supported implementation by communication, tracking and reinforcement mechanisms.

The division's employees then became clearer about their goals and had action plans and mechanisms for tracking and communicating results. This created a more transparent organisation and a belief by all stakeholders that the division was living the value it brought.

Despite the complexity of the situation in this case study, a structured process created a simple focus for everyone involved. This helped people to concentrate on the priorities that mattered. The simple plan was easier to share with other stakeholders and drove clarity and confidence for employees.

Create simplicity to communicate plans to prepare for change.

Be an effective sponsor

In Chapter 1, we defined sponsorship as a leadership role that supports project managers to implement strategic initiatives.

CASE STUDY – CLARIFY SPONSOR MANDATES TO SUSTAIN FOCUS

A local affiliate of a global company wanted to review the way it made decisions and have the right leadership structures for the future. Different forums had been put in place to ensure cross-functional thinking, but the mandate and composition of these forums had evolved and their value had become unclear. The leader foresaw many changes in the environment that would require decision making to be clear, inclusive and effective, so forums with clear mandates would be important.

The current strengths and challenges of the existing teams and changes in the external environment were collected and consolidated from the leadership teams and employee groups. The leadership team and other senior leaders created a framework for future decision making, clarifying the roles of project sponsors and leaders through a series of workshops. One of the key decisions they made was to have a project sponsor who was not the project leader's immediate boss.

The organisation worked effectively within the new framework. Projects were moved forward, and the sponsors and project leaders stepped up to their roles and increased their cross-functional thinking capabilities. They maintained focus on priorities despite many changes in the environment.

This organisation exemplified the importance of clarifying the interaction between sponsors and project managers, and demonstrated that the role of project sponsor is crucial for success. In change-management methodologies, leaders' roles are interchanged with the sponsor designation, as for any specific project you need effective sponsorship to manage the change. According to Prosci, a leading organisation in research change management, sponsors have three key roles in project change.[13] They need to:

- Advocate the change

- Build a coalition across the organisation

- Communicate the change

You need to understand how you can effectively sponsor change. Have a sponsor contract with your project lead which defines who is going to do what and how you will all interact. Make sure you are clear about your role as a sponsor to enable project managers to succeed before you start to implement.

Influence without authority

One of the biggest challenges for any leader is to influence others who don't report to you. If you can, build trusting relationships with others before you need their support so that they will listen to you when you do need it.

Here are some tips for influencing others on a specific change:

- Ensure you are clear about what it is you are asking for. Describe the change from the other person's perspective and explain why it is important for them (and the broader organisation). Can you involve key stakeholders in creating the change you want to make?

- Map out who you need to influence. List who will be impacted by the change and how they will be impacted. Identify who you need to focus on.

- Understand the other person's frame of reference. Think about their context, why they might be supportive, what they would see as benefits, what barriers they may see and how you might overcome those. Think about their preferred communication style so you can approach people in a way they like to be engaged.

- Identify who else they are influenced by. This is especially important if you haven't got a strong relationship. Identify people who are close to the other person and will support the change you are proposing.

- Develop an action plan that moves them along the journey from being aware of the change to being its supporter or advocate.

Influencing others across the organisation is a key part of leading change, so acquiring the skills and tools that enable this is critical.

Key takeaways

- Listen to others' perspectives to bring them on the journey and get a better outcome.

- When the environment is changing around you, take time with your team to reflect and realign. This will reduce the feeling of being overwhelmed and increase feelings of being in control.

- Decide on an approach that suits where you are as an organisation to make sure that it is both efficient and appropriately stretching.

- Improve focus and alignment within your team to accelerate the value you bring to your stakeholders.

- When you plan, look for opportunities to create a sense of autonomy and control for those impacted by change.

- Ensure you have simple messages so everyone can understand the outputs of your plan.

- Clarify a leader's role as a sponsor and give them the tools they need for success.

- Choose how to change to create an environment for creative and open dialogue.

4
Have A Facilitator

What happens if you feel you don't have the time or the skills to structure and facilitate a process that is right for you? How can you partner to access these skills?

This chapter describes the third success factor, having a facilitator. I will demonstrate the value of facilitation along with the different approaches that facilitators use, so you can decide whether to employ the services of a facilitator or develop and use these skills yourself.

Partner with a facilitator

A tough time facilitated

A few years ago, my mum died, and my sisters and I were left with some complex decisions to make. My elder sister wisely suggested that maybe we needed a facilitator. I looked at her in astonishment – hadn't we both spent a lot of our professional lives being facilitators? Another of my sisters had been a head teacher, so she also had strong management skills. Surely, we could do this by ourselves.

It soon hit me that she was absolutely right, and it was one of the best decisions we'd made in years of making tough decisions. Our skilled facilitator guided us through some emotional times. Through the process, we ended up being one of the most high-performing groups I have seen, a credit to both our facilitator and, of course, my family of sisters.

Do you need a facilitator? 'If I'm a good leader, I don't need a facilitator' is one perspective. A facilitator can be seen as an unnecessary luxury. If your meetings are simple and the content is not emotionally or politically charged, as a leader, you can take the facilitation role as well as owning the meeting. However, a changing business environment which is more complex and demanding higher productivity is driving the need to have better-facilitated meetings.

Enable great results

In the Introduction, I defined facilitation as 'Enabling meetings to be successful by running the group process, allowing team leaders and participants to focus on the content of the meeting'. Facilitation can take many forms, so what does great facilitation look like?

As a participant in a well-facilitated meeting, you will feel safe to express your thoughts, and you can concentrate on making the best decisions as you don't have to think about managing time or ensuring good participation. This is clearly demonstrated in my personal story as I worked alongside my sisters through a tough time in our lives with the support of a great facilitator. Bad facilitation shows up when you've given someone else the job of facilitating, but you feel like you have to keep jumping in.

Here are some top tips from organisational leaders I have worked with about what constitutes good facilitation:

- Listen to everyone on the team, ask pertinent questions to draw out relevant and crucial details.

- Pay attention to the detail and nuances of what people say and engage team members so each of their voices is heard.

- Bring focus to the issues that enable the team to work better together.

- Be objective so you can pull together the team's ideas and reflect them back in a non-threatening way to challenge them to do more.

- Help the team to uncover key issues and opportunities within the business.

- Work with the team to find what it really needs, then provide the structure, patience and flexibility to drive tangible results.

- Challenge the team to set goals that are realistic and attainable.

- Guide the team through daunting tasks, which seem to be mired with varying opinions and a myriad of data, by giving them a process.

Enabling leaders to drive strategic change using facilitation creates a pathway to success. It involves structuring the agenda, involving participants and focusing on the outcome of the meeting. Critically, if you are partnering with a good facilitator, they will be able to identify what is needed to complement your style of leading meetings and work with you to ensure successful outcomes.

Use facilitator techniques to engage your team

You will be most effective as a leader if you use facilitative techniques to engage your team. Even without a facilitator, you can create environments where real engagement can happen.

Here are some of the facilitative techniques you can use:

- Co-create an operating framework or terms of reference with your team. Once a team knows its boundaries and its purpose, that creates a certainty which the team is comfortable operating within. Now you can work together to define behaviours and ways of working.

- Keep quiet. Only give advice/insights if you are asked or if participants are missing a critical piece of information. Wait until you're sure they are not going to come up with solutions themselves, and then ask permission if you still want to share. You may be pleasantly surprised with their insights and ideas.

- Ask open-ended questions like 'What would that look like?' and 'What else?' questions. Get the team to ask questions. I attended an innovation session run by Your Business Partner[14] for the Healthcare Businesswomen's Association. The methodology included brainstorming fifty questions that we wanted to ask about the problem. This unleashed a barrage of questions which pushed participants' thinking and enabled us to create some great solutions.

- Help the team identify their individual and team strengths. Use tools like Strengths Finder,[15] or simply identify what individuals in the team are good at. This will enable them to use their strengths to achieve goals, rather than simply following detailed instructions.

Decide if you need an external facilitator

Provide the space for meaningful conversations

Two partners of a consulting business asked me to help them work through a plan for their future. Like the situation with my sisters many years later, I pushed back and asked if they really needed my support. Couldn't they just sit down and discuss it between themselves?

During my one-on-one meetings, and in our one-day structured workshop, I saw the value of an objective third-party asking questions to allow the partners to focus on their individual perspectives. It provided the space for them to have meaningful and productive conversations.

Why is facilitation so important when you develop strategy and lead change? Developing strategy starts with understanding where you are today. There can be a lot of emotion associated with identifying internal and external issues that your organisation is facing, and if you are then setting strategy, describing a vision of what tomorrow could look like is not easy when a group has many different perspectives on each topic. Having someone whose role it is to focus purely on the group process can be valuable.

Like other business skills, facilitating a meeting is something that you can develop with experience. As a leader, when should you go it alone?

- When the problem is simple. Simple problems often need a simple process to resolve them. You just need to get a few people around a table, define the problem, come up with ideas and agree who will action them. This kind of problem tends not to be cross functional in nature, so you'll probably already have some good ideas on how you can resolve it. Maybe you don't even need a meeting.

- When you just need to inform. You may already have defined a way forward, so you simply need to inform others about what is going on. Get the group together so they can develop or take on tasks that are needed to deliver solutions. You don't need to change the way they are working or get buy-in significantly.

- When your group is high performing. If a group has been working together for a while and has implicit or explicit ways of working, each member comes well prepared with a clear outcome in mind for their portion of the agenda. They all complete actions between meetings and the purpose of the meeting is clear.

- When your team shares the role a facilitator usually takes, each member is able to shoulder part of the load of running the meeting. For example, if you as a leader are focusing on ensuring the outcome of the meeting is reached, who is:

  - Visibly recording key points / actions during the meeting?

  - Keeping time?

  - Checking that the group is sticking to the agreed behaviours and ways of working (eg not going off topic or 'down rabbit holes')?

- When you actively design your meetings and have little stake in the outcome.

If you are going to facilitate yourself, think about what each meeting needs, and then how you will get there most effectively using the range of tools you have seen work before. Design the right process to match the desired meeting output and consider the pre-work you need to do to have an effective meeting. Recognise that when you convene a group of people, you are using their precious time, so plan the meeting accordingly. In the meeting, you then don't need to direct the content and can focus on ensuring all voices are heard.

When your problems are simple, you don't need group buy-in, your groups are high performing and you are skilled in group processes, then you do not need facilitation support.

Use different approaches to engage large groups

There are many reasons why facilitation is growing in importance. These include the complexity of the challenges that organisations face, the constant change and churn in teams, the need to take into account cross-functional and diverse opinions, and the absolute essential of employee engagement. Leaders need to be participants who are fully engaged in content and decision making, not focusing on using the right process.

Meetings are important to involve and hear all stakeholder views, and now more than ever, there is pressure to use people's time effectively. No one has the time to sit in a meeting where they are not engaged and feel like they could be doing something more valuable. Good facilitation enables strong engagement.

Virtual meetings using technology are an important way of doing business as they allow meetings between participants in different locations, so tools like Zoom, Skype and WebEx are now mainstream. Great facilitation is even more important when your teams are meeting via technology as engaging people who aren't in the same room is challenging. In Chapter 8, we will look at tips on how to hold great meetings. There are some additional technical tools you need to be successful in virtual meetings, but the basic skill-sets are important no matter the medium.

There are a number of processes that are helpful to engage large groups of people. For example, use world cafés[16] to ask critical questions that many people can answer. A world café involves moving participants around 'table groups' so that cross fertilisation of ideas can occur and common themes emerge.

More sophisticated and structured is the use of an approach known as Syntegration, and I have been lucky enough to have had a long association with the Syntegrity Group. What this group does using the formula of Cracking Complexity is special.[17] Their 'cutting-edge, highly engaging, step-by-step formula for cracking incredibly knotty and important challenges in mere days, whilst mobilizing those who must execute' has shown benefits for organisations globally.

The premise is that simple problems require a low number of people's perspectives to resolve, but as problems become more complex, they require a greater diversity of perspectives. To manage large groups of people with those diverse perspectives, the group brings in a team of facilitators who operate within a structured process. This allows participants to focus on answering a big question without having to be concerned about the process of getting there. Organisations that have worked with the group are in no doubt that facilitation brings huge value.

In the increasingly connected world, facilitation is important to enable diverse groups of people to solve complex problems.

Key takeaways

- Use a facilitator when your problems are complex, you need group buy-in, your group is not high performing and you are not skilled in group processes.

- Focus on content by having a great facilitator who concentrates on the process of the meetings.

- Use facilitative skills to engage your team. Create operating frameworks, ask questions and understand team strengths.

- Use a facilitator with groups that are working through highly emotional subjects or in large groups of people who are addressing complex issues.

5
Involve people

Involving people early is one of the most important success factors in leading change. All you need to do is ensure that they:

- Understand the current state is not a good place to be

- See that the future is much more appealing

- Have a clear pathway to move from one place to another

Simple? It takes an upfront investment in time, but it is one that will pay off when you need to implement a change. If the change will have a big impact and the environment is stressed, you need to make this investment as early as you can.

The first thing you need to do is decide how much involvement of various stakeholders you need. This chapter explores how you can involve people who will be impacted by change, including employees, peers and customers, and recommends some useful tools that you can use to increase engagement and motivation to act.

See through others' eyes

The benefits of having leaders who appreciate the value of preparing for change and taking the change through to effective implementation can be seen through the lenses of different stakeholders.

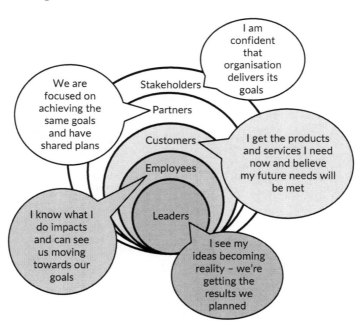

Day to day, the tensions of different stakeholders' needs can become apparent. A strategic view where all stakeholder perspectives are part of your organisation vision is the way to achieve sustainable success.

Leaders want to see their ideas turned into results. Employees want to grow and feel valued for their efforts. Customers want products or services that bring value to them. Suppliers or partners want to grow with the organisation. Shareholders or funders want to see a return on their investment. By looking through the eyes of others when you are planning or in day-to-day work, you are constantly building a strategic perspective.

Use environmental scanning

CASE STUDY - EXTERNAL SCANNING LEADS TO CHANGE

A university needed to create a value proposition as part of its efforts to attract funding for its research. It was becoming critical that the university partnered with industry to either get funding directly or get government funding.

Not all of the research scientists saw the need to do this. When I asked each individual researcher about the environment they worked in, they demonstrated that their biggest concern was that the time they could devote to doing research was continually shrinking. They were focusing on their internal challenges, but

> when I shared the environmental scan and the best practices of others back with the group, they committed to engaging with their external community and enabling value propositions.

One of the oldest tools in the strategic planning armoury is to conduct an environmental scan. Look at your external (political, economic, social and technological) and internal environment, and use this scan as a base from which to plan your future. This will enable you to step back and look at your current state and how you are competing.

A SWOT analysis[18] (see Chapter 1) is a good way to summarise what you have learned from an environmental scan. This could be seen as a purely logical process step, but its real value lies in the engagement that you create by getting everyone's input and helping them to see the bigger picture they are operating in.

What makes an environmental scan such an engaging way to start any change process?

- You create the 'Why change?' argument. A powerful motivation is understanding what is happening that could cause problems unless you change (ie a 'burning platform'[19]).

- You start to engage different individuals or groups of individuals by collecting data and opinions, so they are actively considering what needs to be done next and are better prepared for action planning.

- You build strategic thinking capability. By putting themselves in the shoes of others in their environment, people see things in a different way. By considering external as well as internal environments, they step out of their day-to-day thinking. A useful tip is to rearrange the traditional SWOT and create an opportunities, threats, strengths, weaknesses (OTSW)[20] matrix, to make external thinking the first priority. This is important for two reasons: it is often the external environment that will force or enable change internally, and you may otherwise miss something that could make you uncompetitive or obsolete if you ignore it.

- You create balance between positive and negative thinking. It's easier to think about the threats and weaknesses you need to fix. By thinking about opportunities first, and then threats and strengths before weaknesses, you create energy and recognition for what is present. Appreciative Inquiry[21] and strengths[22] based thinking are concepts which describe in more detail why focusing on the positive is so important. But do capture negative perspectives to allow people to express their concerns and use them as drivers of change to move away from the current state.

- Consider using challenges to engage a group rather than painfully picking out weaknesses, which can be perceived as criticism, so an OTSW becomes an OTSC matrix.

- Create a summary via an OTSC matrix to enable engagement of a group. The complete scan with every perspective can be overwhelming, so summarise with three to five points for each quadrant. This makes further prioritisation easier.

Inspire through a vision

Rallying the troops

My early days learning about leadership seemed to be focused on the opinion that a great leader creates inspirational visions that make others want to follow them. I always struggled with this; maybe I could never be a good leader as I just didn't have what it took to inspire others to follow me in the way that Shakespeare's rallying 'Once more unto the breach' call did in Henry V. [23]

Many years later, I realised that a rallying call is just a small part of engaging and inspiring people.

It's great if you put into words what a clear picture of the future looks like, but it is even more inspiring to team members if they can see their own thoughts and words incorporated into a vision. In Chapter 1, we defined a vision as 'a description of what your organisation will become in a set timeframe'. Creating a vision with your team that is aligned to both a broader organisational vision and an individual's personal purpose is key to achieving the focus and energy that will lead to success.

How do you co-create a vision with your team that will truly inspire them? Here are four pointers for success:

- Understand why staying with the status quo isn't the best option. Use an OTSC matrix or other approaches to help people understand that the world is changing and the impact of staying still. This creates an incentive for them to input into a future direction.

- Understand individual and team motivations for success. By understanding and tapping into individual aspirations, you create more engagement in driving towards a future that will achieve not only team goals, but also those of individuals. There is a reason they are doing the job they are doing.

- Explore team and individual values. Define the common values the team believe are important to encapsulate that will be at the heart of your future success. It's insightful to see these commonalities.

- See your team through others' eyes. Imagine what your customers or other stakeholders would value.

Once you've done this, you will be ready to create thematic statements that will include each stakeholder's perspective, your own ideas and those of team members. Craft a vision statement where each word reflects the themes you have identified. Share it with other stakeholders and refine it, if needed, so that it really expresses where you want to go.

By using these points, you and your team will feel real ownership of the vision, and then all you need to do is move towards it.

Use future business modelling

CASE STUDY – CREATING A NEW BUSINESS MODEL

A small company had developed its vision and value proposition but wanted to explore different options for bringing its services to markets and what resources it would use to do that. Using the concepts described in Business Model Generation,[24] the leadership team mapped out what they could do, and then used that map to prioritise the best opportunities and how they would resource these activities. This allowed them to envisage the detail they needed to move towards the vision they had created. It also gave them the clarity and alignment they needed as they saw how the organisation would work in the future.

Finding the words to describe a future state sometimes isn't enough. The leadership team in the case study defined their vision statement (a description of what the organisation would become in a set time-frame) and value proposition (what it would deliver to specified customers), but they wanted to get more detailed and envision how this would really work.

This is what a business model does. At its core is the value proposition of the company, but it also looks at two other major aspects:

- The resources needed to deliver the value proposition (the people, partners, processes and systems)

- How revenue will be generated (the channels to go to market, who customers will be, market segments, and how sales will be achieved)

By looking at these aspects, you can evaluate what needs to change to realise a new value proposition, or to deliver on an existing one. Creating a vision with your team is inspiring for everyone. Using tools like Business Model Generation makes the vision concrete.

Use scenario planning

What can you do as a leader if your future is not clear? Sometimes there is so much uncertainty in the world that it is hard to define what the future will look like. A planning tool that has proved successful when there has been significant change is scenario planning.[25]

CASE STUDY – MENTALLY PREPARING FOR CHANGES

A division of a large multinational knew that changes were coming but didn't know what the direction would be. The divisional leadership team wanted to make sure the staff were well prepared, so whatever change was made globally, they would be able to respond effectively. They were concerned that doing nothing to prepare would see them in a poor position to respond quickly.

They created various scenarios that described potential future operating models and the division's role within them. Then they examined each model within a team workshop and developed plans to address these potential diverse outcomes. Sharing each plan, they identified trigger points that would help the group to respond. The leadership team saw that a few basic actions would be useful across all scenarios (eg building an inventory of the team's strengths that could be shared with new senior leaders).

Subsequently, the team members were mentally prepared for whatever changes came their way; they felt more in control. Identification of trigger points enabled them to quickly move into response mode. One of the scenarios that they had created was exactly what transpired, so the teams were nowhere near as overwhelmed as they might otherwise have been.

Involving your team in mapping out various potential scenarios is a great way to prepare for the future and feel confident that you are ready for whatever may emerge. By recognising the trigger points that mean you are moving towards one of the scenarios, you can respond quickly and put in place the plans that you have already prepared.

Engage your peers

The importance of building strong cross-functional partnerships

I had just taken on the role of operations director after many years as a consultant, and I realised that cross-functional cooperation was going to be important when I got back from holiday to find one of my team members wanting to see me on an urgent matter. Another department wasn't cooperating and I needed to sort it out with the manager – a new peer of mine.

When I went to see her, she had a different perspective. After an initial conversation, we decided we needed to go to our boss to get a judgement (how often does this happen?). He said we needed to figure it out between us, so we involved our teams and agreed how we could work together for the good of the organisation.

Finding a common purpose was key, as was our willingness to build a strong partnership. We decided we would have regular meetings to ensure that we addressed issues early, and she became a great sounding board for me with her strong skills in people management. I had relearned the lesson of building strong relationships with colleagues, ideally before you need their support.

Many years later, I was talking with a vice president who was sponsoring the implementation of a new system, and he described the lack of buy-in he was experiencing. We identified the crucial role that he needed to play by engaging his peers as secondary sponsors, as without their support, the new system he was implementing would not work.

The expectation that sponsors have peer support needs to be explicit, as often that engagement does not happen naturally. Building relationships across functions before you need support is critical to accelerate implementation.

Talk to your customers strategically

Strategic input for future growth

One company I worked with wanted to engage its customers differently. In the past, the teams had sent out a satisfaction survey which had asked customers how well they rated the quality of the company's product. This time, the teams had a discussion with their most important customers about what they saw changing in the business and what might be needed in the future.

This changed the relationship in many ways. The company's teams started to be seen as partners rather than suppliers, which added more value as they developed products for the future. The range of services the company was considered for increased as these customer discussions opened opportunities. They also gave the company's teams valuable information about the future competition they might be facing and how they could position themselves more effectively. The teams did get information about how well they were currently doing, but the increased strategic input allowed them to explore solutions with their customers that enabled future growth.

Too often, the conversations you have with your customers are based on satisfaction with your products or services rather than how you could more effectively work together. Talk to them about their future so you build your business to address their needs.

Open out engagement

One of the biggest decisions an organisation makes is how widely to open out its strategic planning and preparation for change. Conceptually, opening out engagement to the whole organisation and relevant stakeholders would lead to maximum engagement (and therefore easier and speedier implementation). It would also increase strategic thinking capability throughout the organisation. Practically, this can be challenging.

There are many ways that organisations have found to push their boundaries and increase engagement without becoming overwhelmed with information. When you prepare for change, this decision can be made using the tips we explored in Chapter 3, like the maturity vs complexity matrix.

You can use other approaches that involve large groups of people, like world cafés and the Syntegrity approach described in Chapter 4. Curate online data to produce compelling insights using tools such as the Hot Spots Movement.[26] These kinds of approaches are especially useful in complex situations when you need to hear from many stakeholder groups.

There are also tools and techniques that can be incorporated in a top-down planning process to increase engagement. Telling people the direction of change and asking how it can be implemented is one way of creating engagement. Another is to set boundaries and ask people to fill in the detail.

Use sticky notes in many parts of your change process to get input and ideas from others. Ask a question and get people to respond on sticky notes to generate ideas. Group these ideas and ask people to vote to create clear priorities before devising an action plan.

This approach to brainstorming is powerful because:

- You allow everyone to put forward their own ideas and thoughts without being shot down by others (agree that rule first).

- People can write down what they think without a facilitator or leader translating it on to a flip chart.

- It levels the playing field – it's not about the loudest voice or quickest thinker, or the hierarchy of the organisation. You'll hear from the quieter colleagues in your group.

- Sticky notes posted on a flip chart or whiteboard create a visual reminder, which aids people's understanding of ideas rather than them relying on what they have heard (or not).

Using sticky notes can be even more effective if you:

- Go slowly – allow everyone quiet time after posing the question so that they can generate thoughtful insights. This can be challenging to do, especially for impatient people who just want to move forward.

- Go anonymously – this can free people up to speak their truth about how to solve an issue or identify the real issue in the first place.

- Go strategically – enable understanding of all perspectives by taking the time to group and identify priorities versus debating and getting stuck in 'analysis-paralysis' mode. This leads to a broader view and creates more ideas and a clearer path forward.

- Go quickly – use an electronic brainstorming tool like vWall[27] so transcription errors and the effort required to write the ideas up are reduced, and quicker consolidation of results is possible. This allows you to collect ideas remotely or before or after a work session, which can then be displayed to everyone involved and recorded easily. It is also environmentally friendly.

A Harvard article[28] showed that incorporating these ideas, ie giving people time to think and allowing anonymity via online brainstorming, not only yielded 70–100% more ideas, but the quality of those ideas was higher than they had been before.

Key takeaways

- Scan your environment by involving teams and broader organisational stakeholders. This will build momentum towards a new vision.

- Create a vision with your team to inspire them. Use tools like Business Model Generation to make a vision concrete. Use scenario planning if your future is not clear.

- Build relationships across functions before you need others' support to accelerate implementation.

- Talk to your customers about their future so you can build your future to address their needs.

- Use simple tools like sticky notes to enable diverse voices to be heard.

- Consider sophisticated large-group processes when you need to solve complex issues and mobilise many stakeholders for future change.

6

Make Differences Work

If people with different backgrounds and thinking styles work together effectively, it can create a unique and competitive future. But this is not an easy thing to achieve as:

- Different personalities and perspectives can bring conflict.

- Organisational barriers need to be overcome when you are working together across functions or with different organisations.

This chapter explores the fifth success factor in change: how you can harness the different skillsets and perspectives that people bring, enabling you to realise long-term success through working together. It is important as a leader of change to ensure momentum and focus on the desired future.

Build a team of different individuals

Differences lead to breakthroughs

I remember one of the first personality tests I did.[29] I was one of four conservative scientists who had just joined a group of innovative and creative engineers. The test results showed that the four of us were in the bottom-right corner of the matrix, ie 'Analysing – methodical, principled and accurate', and the engineers were in the top-left, ie 'Promoting – creative enthusiastic and spontaneous'.

We spent a lot of time in a workshop practising how to talk to each other. The exciting journey that we went on as a team was remarkable as we analysts increasingly valued the creative energy of the engineers, and they appreciated the logical thinking we brought. The breakthroughs in design that we made many years ago can still be seen today.

The acceptance that diversity and inclusion are important and have a strong relationship to business success is becoming more established.[30] Whether it's gender, age, race, brain diversity, culture or different experiences that people have, many viewpoints around a business table, if harnessed well, will lead to more creativity and ultimately better business results. Achieving diversity is a goal many organisations are striving for with the hope that when they have achieved this, results will follow. But it's not quite as easy as this, is it?

The more different individuals there are in a team, the more risk there is of disagreement, which then requires time and debate to resolve and agree on the best solution. If you invest in this debate and openness, it will strengthen your chances of success. If you surround yourself with similar people, you run the risk of tunnel vision, ultimately leading to failure or underachievement.

Harness differences

If you have made the effort to have a diverse team, how can you harness the differences you have around the table to achieve better results? There are many concepts and tools to help leaders build high-performing teams, but you can lay a foundation by helping individuals feel safe and providing practical actions.

Create a safe environment

Work has been done by Google and others[31] that shows one of the key ingredients to high-performing teams is that individuals can voice their opinions safely. If you are leading change, people who are impacted need to raise their concerns so that each one can be addressed. It might be that there aren't easy solutions, but often people find just being listened to is enough. Sometimes others can identify a solution or reassure their teammates.

If you create an environment where people feel that their team is the best space to share issues and address their collective concerns, that is powerful and engaging. You will build forward momentum.

Create an effective team

Once you have an environment in which all team members feel safe to express themselves, you need to create an effective team. Here are five simple steps that you can use to turn a group of different people into that team, making their differences work:

- Understand each other's skills, backgrounds and motivations. You'll reach a common understanding more quickly and be able to make decisions more effectively. Whether you use Myers Briggs,[32] Hermann Brain Dominance,[33] DISC[34] or other strength profilers, understand the similarities and differences in a group to create:

  - A common language

  - An understanding of the need for flexibility

  - A framework for dialogue

- Understand your common purpose. It is critical that teams have a common purpose, so facilitate your team to develop and crystallise this together. Connect their personal purpose to the team purpose. People don't need to have the same personal purpose, but aligning behind a common team purpose will bring them together.

- Create your vision. Along with describing a common purpose, create an inspiring vision to bring different people together, as we discussed in Chapter 5. Create goals (measures that you have achieved your vision) together to enable buy-in.

- Agree the behaviours you will adopt and demonstrate as a team. This aspect is fundamental for any team's success. Review the behaviours you need for successful meetings and hold each other accountable. Use your organisation or team values as a start point and ask how you will demonstrate those values. Make it concrete by considering how you will share tasks or airtime. Alternatively, decide how you need to behave for a specific meeting to be successful.

- Agree when you will meet and for how long. Exploring practicalities will help your team to feel secure, knowing that the work you do in your time together will continue.

These tools provide a good foundation to harness differences and become a high-performing team that delivers results.

Focus on strengths

CASE STUDY – USING TEAM STRENGTHS IN TIMES OF UNCERTAINTY

A team in a pharmaceutical organisation was waiting for an acquisition to take place. Their future, as a team and as individuals, was uncertain. They had previously worked on long-term plans that were focused on using their strengths to maximise their value to their internal customers, but it didn't make sense to work on long-term plans when the acquiring company might have other plans.

A workshop focused on how to use their strengths in times of uncertainty. They shared their individual perspectives of mergers and what could happen. They also re-shared their strengths and identified those behaviours that would help them be resilient through the waiting period, as well as preparing for their individual futures.

As a result, the team members were better prepared for the period of uncertainty and were able to refer to the helpful behaviours they had identified. They felt they had the support of the team and their leader in managing ongoing changes. They also had individual resources that they could use if they needed to interview for future roles.

As well as focusing on strengths as part of an organisational environmental scan, think about how individual strengths contribute to a team's strengths. This is a great way to harness and appreciate the team members' differences, as well as the similarities you have in a team. Marcus Buckingham's definition of strength as something that gives you energy and weakness as what drains you is useful here.[35]

Having a team that focuses on strengths to get results means you have a highly motivated and engaged team. You do have to do tasks, either as individuals or as a team, that are not to your strengths, but you can minimise the time you spend on these tasks to be more energised and productive.

Managing weaknesses for success

One team I worked with looked at their strengths and identified that, as a group, they were missing the strength of recording and following through on their actions. 'Thank goodness we have you for these critical meetings,' they said. I then let them know that it is not a strength of mine, either, but I have learned to be good at it as I know it is critical for my success and that of the teams I work with. If I had to do this all the time, it would be exhausting.

What motivates me when I'm working with teams is making links between different thoughts, people and ideas, and having insights. Using me in this way would provide a much more powerful strength and resource for the team, but it was important to realise that we could manage weaknesses in different ways.

Knowing your strengths and weaknesses enables you and your team to harness the strengths and manage the weaknesses.

Harnessing the strengths of a network

As an independent consultant, I have a great network of people who complement what I do. The network includes different technical skills, like performance management, or communications and training consultants, and different ways of working. We cover many spectrums, from detail orientation to conceptual thinking, structured to creative. When we harness group thinking and bring it to bear on problems we may be having as individuals, the people we work with benefit from a combination of strengths.

Seek out people who complement your skills rather than being the same as you. This can be powerful and lead to breakthrough thinking.

Embrace cross functionality

Beware the silo

Many times, in different corporations, I have found myself in a silo. For me, this has been within an R&D function where scientists are rightly proud of the excellent work they do, but don't always value the other parts of the organisation like manufacturing (where 'they just make products') or sales and marketing (which is 'all about talking a good line').

This is a tongue-in-cheek perspective and is not true for everyone in an organisation, and neither is the stereotype of the R&D department ('they have no communication skills or understanding of the real world'). But unfortunately, people can become too comfortable in their silo.

Working with others outside a silo who are a little different to you doesn't happen naturally and tensions can build up. It can be hard to remember to do this when you want to get things done quickly. There is a natural reaction to turn inward and have fewer outward-facing discussions.

Within a work silo, you are with groups of people who echo your views and perspectives. It's easier to have a conversation if you can understand where someone is coming from (ie they have the same background) or you like them. Unfortunately, this can channel your thinking in one direction and stifle broader strategic understanding, which does not lead easily to creating unique value. Actively seeking out people who have different perspectives has many advantages, especially when you want to lead change that impacts a broad range of people.

Develop collaborative senior leadership teams

CASE STUDY – COLLABORATION AND ALIGNMENT IN A TIME OF TRANSITION

A growing biotech was transitioning from a R&D and scale-up to a commercial organisation. New products were emerging from the pipeline, additional facilities were being built and employee numbers were significantly increasing. The organisation needed to drive towards a more cohesive and clear future, and to have a plan that could be communicated and delivered to shareholders, employees and the external world. In doing so, the leadership team wanted to maintain their collaborative and valued ways of working.

By moving through a process of collecting information from key executive team leaders on their current state, holding a workshop with the extended leadership team to prioritise key issues, creating a clear vision and developing behaviours that the executive team would demonstrate to show their values, they began the process of transitioning to a new organisation. Their commitment to collaborate and be aligned served them well as they made this transition.

Senior leadership teams can have the most diverse functional perspectives in an organisation (whether they are the most diverse in other ways is still a work in progress), but it is critical that they work together, otherwise functional barriers will become apparent. Doing this successfully will result in clear and aligned leadership. This builds confidence and sets the groundwork for cross-functional collaboration. Strong results follow.

CASE STUDY – BECOMING AN EFFECTIVE CROSS-FUNCTIONAL LEADERSHIP TEAM

An established sales and marketing organisation wanted to change its ways of working to be more collaborative. The leadership team had developed a vision and strategic initiatives, and needed support and focus to bring this to life. They needed to change their ways of working from short-term crisis management to long-term proactive planning and thinking. Each of the leaders had different strengths and capabilities to make this come to life, so the organisation wanted to see measurable results from their planning exercise.

Each member of the leadership team took time to review their landscape. The results were consolidated in a joint summary to allow them to confirm which strategic initiatives were valid. These initiatives were prioritised and ownership for each (cross-functional) imperative was assigned.

Each leader received tailored support to further develop initiatives and supplement their skills. For one leader, this support focused on increasing his long-term thinking; for another, it helped her to identify how she would measure success. Another needed support in how he could present his thoughts to his peers in an impactful manner. One leader needed coaching on how he would engage with his peers in developing and implementing his initiative. Another leader, who was more experienced in doing this kind of work, provided insights that the others could use. By helping to grow the skills of each leader, the support made sure that collaboration became easy and the overall team leader was able to focus on the content of the plans rather than having to coach each team member individually.

Each leader continued to develop their initiatives, creating practical action plans and measures for them, and an overall scorecard to measure results. The leadership team became engaged in implementing their strategy. Teamwork increased due to a clear focus, and individual capabilities in strategy implementation developed. A shift to long-term thinking emerged by the leaders keeping track through scorecards and integrating strategic discussions into their team meetings. Together, they learned to become a true leadership team rather than senior representatives of their individual functions.

Patrick Lencioni talks about which team is the most important for senior leaders.[36] His insight that the number-one team should be the one you sit on as a leader is impactful. Follow this advice to create a collaborative organisation.

If a leadership team isn't aligned, then those reporting to the individual leaders will compare notes and become confused and disgruntled that the company's direction and purpose aren't clear. The concept of the shadow of the leader plays out with employees adopting the behaviours that they see in their leaders.[37] If you value your departmental interests more than cross-functional collaboration, then this behaviour will be seen across the organisation, not just at the leadership level. If you build trusting collaborative relationships in leadership teams, these are likely to be played out in the organisation.

Make mergers and acquisitions successful

CASE STUDY – CRUCIAL COMMUNICATIONS

Post-merger of two organisations, a division needed to establish the new organisation's vision, strategic initiatives and ways of working. Ownership of the resulting plan was critical for the leadership team so they could renew and revisit it on an annual basis, communicating it to key stakeholders so they could receive the resources they needed to be successful.

They took the time to participate in a workshop, with the leader and the human resources representative playing key roles, to develop a long-term plan and a strong leadership team. This was followed up with support to translate strategic initiatives into action plans and agreed mechanisms to track progress at leadership team meetings. The leadership team selected and applied tools for specific strategic initiatives, eg an influencing plan, project management techniques and business case development. Then they engaged managers and employees in this new direction, so everyone knew what they needed to do to embrace the new ways of working.

The leadership team established a sustainable renewal process of strategy development and implementation. On an annual basis, they updated their environmental scan, strategic initiatives and ownership, identifying external and internal best practices to supplement this work. They were engaged in implementing strategy and their teamwork increased. Individual capabilities in strategic thinking and implementation grew.

All stakeholders were aware of the divisional direction and what the leadership team expected. As a result, the divisions received the resources that allowed them to reach their goals.

When companies, teams or departments merge and new functions are created, by default, the teams that have been working together in the past will have different ways of working to the teams of the newly merged organisation. It's critical as a leader of a new team that you take the time to state your purpose and how you will be working together. This adds clarity within the team, and to your customers, partners and peer groups. If you do this well, your team will be motivated and ready to start working on your new mandate, as well as building a solid basis for the future.

Create brilliant partnerships

As we discussed in Chapter 2, the need to work with partners is becoming ever more critical. Take a strategic, collaborative view of this.

Pay attention to be brilliant

If working across organisations in a cross-functional way is hard, then working with your external partners could be harder. This is because:

- Organisations have different goals to each other.

- Size differences can cause conflict, with smaller organisations able to move and change direction more quickly than larger ones.

- If a larger organisation is supplying a smaller organisation, it can get frustrated with the changing demands of its more agile partner.

Paradoxically, people who spend time at partner interfaces find that crossing this barrier is sometimes easier than working with their internal colleagues. This is because the technical skills and backgrounds of individuals at the interface may be similar, so they understand what each other does. Whatever the situation, you need to continue to pay attention to these relationships and maintain a trusting and collaborative partnership.

Build long-term partnerships

Just as cross-functional teams set up joint goals and principles or ways of working, it's important that your partnerships do this too.

CASE STUDY – BRILLIANT PARTNERSHIPS

Leaders of a growing biotech company were reflecting on what capabilities were critical for them to succeed in the future. In an inspirational conversation, they coalesced on the imperative: 'We need to be brilliant partners.'

They went about this by:

- Developing their partnership principles together. This built on the trust they already had, and any issues were turned into a shared positive vision.

- Assessing how they were living these principles. They asked everyone involved in the partnership to rate how they saw the principles being demonstrated day to day. That enabled them to identify the strengths and challenges they had as partners. They prioritised the most important issues.

- Creating actions to address their priorities. They developed ideas to improve their partnership and created actions to address.

- Checking in to deliver continuous improvement. They continued to enhance their partnerships.

It took just a few weeks to complete the first three steps of this process. As a result, there was an increased and, thanks to the ongoing check-ins, lasting commitment to success on both sides.

By identifying your critical partnerships and following these simple steps, you can create successful long-term partnerships.

Build a network

Networking externally and internally

Networking has been a critical part of my success in the latter years of my career as I have been able to bring resources and ideas to situations that needed different skillsets. But this hasn't only been true for my time as an external consultant looking for work. My connections across a corporation enabled me to pull on resources that I didn't work with on a day-to-day basis. Rather than using external resources, I was able to tap into another part of the organisation and partner with people there. This had the added advantage of them knowing the organisation already and bringing relevant examples and experience to the table.

Giving generously to my network has resulted in my network helping me. Certainly, the best networkers I know are always considering how to help the other person first and embrace the value of mutuality.

Saying thank you and appreciating what others have done for you, even if you can't return the favour immediately, is a critical part of effective networking. Whether you are networking to find your next career move or a potential business partner, or simply to gain external perspective, learning how to do it well is a critical skill in this ultra-connected world. In the past, networking was done by keeping in touch with your old school or university friends, but if you really want to harness differences, then cast a wider net to access a range of resources that you may need in your career.

There are many ways to network. Social media plays a key part, allowing you to keep in touch with colleagues and partners in different ways. Use whatever platform suits your style. Attend (live or virtual) networking events to broaden your thinking and meet new people. Preparing for these events and following up is key. For practical tips, please have a look at my article 'Reducing the fear in networking Part 1: Preparing to network'.[38] If you are clear about your objective, remember that it is a mutually beneficial activity and treat it as one step in the process of building long-term relationships, then you will be set for successful networking.

There are many ways to make differences work, whether you are thinking across functions, at a leadership team level, or with external partners or networks. By capturing different perspectives as an organisation, team or individual, you can be more strategic and tap into resources that can change the way you bring value to the world.

Key takeaways

- Look from the perspective of each stakeholder you engage with. Consider the benefits they will see.

- Create an environment where individuals can raise concerns about change and be involved in how they are resolved.

- Take practical steps to harness differences and build great teamwork.

- Understand and share individual strengths to create an energised team that will also manage weaknesses.

- Consciously seek out different perspectives. Silos happen naturally, as does hiring in your own image. Breakthroughs happen when you harness different perspectives.

- Create an effective leadership team that role models good cross-functional teamwork. If leaders work well together, the organisation's employees will often follow. Create effective team ways of working to enable results.

- Take the time to engage and focus on what is needed when you set up new teams (eg post-merger) so everyone is motivated and working to achieve common goals.

- Think strategically with colleagues in your business and across organisational boundaries with your partners. Take simple steps to grow the strength of your partnerships.

- Build a network to broaden your strategic thinking and find resources that you can involve in leading change.

7
Measure And Monitor Success

How do you, as a leader of change, define what value is? How do you measure change? This chapter describes the sixth success factor in leading for change, the importance of measuring success, explaining how you can overcome barriers to measurement so change is tangible.

'What gets measured gets done' is a long-standing saying that some argue goes back to the fifteenth century. It's hard to disagree with this simple maxim which compels you to measure what you believe is important. And what can be more important than ongoing success? If you are leading change, why wouldn't you want to measure that you are really making a difference from a long-term strategic perspective? But many who have tried to measure this success have found that it is not easy and they have used up valuable time without the return they were looking for.

Understand the barriers

There are many reasons why measuring success is not easy:

- How do you quantify measures that give you confidence that you will achieve long-term success, ensuring you end up with the right quality within agreed budget and to the timeline you have set?

- You need to take responsibility for setting targets and taking action if the targets are not achieved. This can be hard to do as targets are concrete and visible, so people in your team have to feel safe and ready to take this on (more about this in Chapter 9).

- Often meetings are set up to be about how you address issues rather than getting clarity (and agreement) on what the issue is and its impact on success. People can see measurement as bureaucratic if no meaningful actions result.

- It's much easier to set targets and measure current performance rather than how well you are doing against a future vision. While these measurements make it clear what success looks like today, what is relevant today may not be relevant for the future.

- Because it's tough to identify a simple, relevant and pragmatic measure for success, we stop looking. Sometimes the time it takes to collect the data seems to be worth more than the value it brings, and what if the measures you institute drive behaviours that you don't want?

These can be significant hurdles to overcome and it's easy to default to not measuring at all. But despite these challenges, you need to measure success. Here is how you can do that.

Create a compelling story

These are some of the reasons why you need to measure:

- It enables focus on what is important, and focus is critical to success. Having the right outcome measures in place and discussing what you need to do to achieve the targets you set enables true focus and prioritisation.

- It drives more clarity. The journey to creating a measure helps you clarify the end state (even if you and your team don't agree the final measure).

- It improves meeting effectiveness. Imagine having focused meetings that are based on reviewing the impact of your work on success. Having an effective long-term strategic scorecard transforms long process-oriented meetings into action-oriented outcome-focused meetings (more about this in Chapter 8).

- It drives accountability. You need to ensure that each measure is owned by a leader who drives progress towards a target (a measure owner). Their responsibility is to take action to ensure results are meeting targets, which is a simple way of creating accountability. You will be able to recognise success as it is visible, and positive results follow. Note: it is critical that you build a supportive culture where people who are accountable are rewarded for taking visibility and feel comfortable in sharing and asking for support (more in Chapter 9).

- It supports improved cross-functional teamwork. When you develop measures that align with your common purpose, cross-functional teamwork improves. Good measures enable your measure owners to ask for and receive specific support to achieve joint cross-functional goals.

- It quantifies your overall strategy. By defining measures and setting targets that translate your vision into tangible outcomes, you are more likely to achieve your business goals.

The journey to measuring success is worth undertaking as it enhances focus and alignment and creates the results you seek from your strategy. It translates your ideas about a desired future into a concrete vision that can be measured, enabling you to track how you are doing in achieving your vision *and* take action to course correct.

Use a strategic scorecard

CASE STUDY – CHANGING METRICS – CHANGING PERSPECTIVE

A management team in the not-for-profit sector decided to refresh the organisation metrics that they shared with their board of directors. The current metrics were too operational and too detailed for board purposes, leading to confusion, gaps in relevant data and inefficient use of board time. For example, there was a lack of staff/resource deployment measures; revenue sources, particularly from fundraising activities; and client satisfaction/safety measures. Using newly revised metrics, the directors now focus on fewer and longer-term measures. This provides them with a more strategic view of the organisation's health status.

A scorecard is a way for you to get an overview of whether the actions you are taking are leading to success. Unlike a project dashboard, which primarily focuses on whether you have completed actions, a scorecard shows the measures that you have defined as having an impact in moving your organisation to success. It is process, rather than outcome, focused and is complementary to having actions in place.

The balanced scorecard approach was first developed by Kaplan and Norton in 1992.[39] It enables perspectives for different stakeholders to be taken into consideration. Typically, the perspectives it considers are:

- Financial (shareholders or corporate)

- Customers/partners (internal or external customers, end users or consumers)

- Process (critical internal)

- People and learning (employee motivation and capability of employees to deliver)

Thinking about what success would mean from each of these perspectives, you can create great dialogue about the vision of an organisation.

The first step to creating measures is the strategy mapping tool.[40] It maps what is critical from each of the financial, customer/partners, process and people/learning perspectives. By using it, you see how different perspectives can be measured, and it shows the links between each of these different perspectives. You can see how strong people working with effective processes that deliver to satisfied customers lead to healthy financial results. And it doesn't have to be complicated.

Once you have this strategy map, you can create a balanced scorecard. Take each success factor on your strategy map and turn it into measures that you can track over time with targets that show you have reached your goals.

If you develop and use a scorecard regularly, it helps you to understand what is critical for you to sustain success in your team or organisation. The balanced scorecard is a great approach to take as it enables the breadth of thinking you need to incorporate for long-term success.

Apply learning

Considering the barriers that we highlighted at the start of this chapter, you can use these tips to create and implement measurement systems like the balanced scorecard:

- Involve people who can change outcomes in the review of measures. This simple and pragmatic tip means that measures will be useful and will drive actions. If actions are not taken as a result of the review, you need to evaluate if you need them.

- Drive from strategy, be pragmatic in implementation. When you have developed the direction you would like to go in, think about what this would look like from the perspective of each of your key stakeholders. Ask what would be critical to measure and develop measures based on these perspectives. At the same time, think about what is practical, for example what is already in place or easy to collect, and use these measures as a start point.

- Allow continuous refinement to reflect better insight, focus and control. As you develop measures, set targets and collect data, check to see if the measure is meeting its purpose of moving you towards your goals. If it isn't, then refine it or take it off your scorecard. Continue to consider whether you have the right number of measures and if you can reduce them to ensure focus.

- Use scorecards to drive agendas and actions as a powerful enabler of culture. If measures are not used to support culture, then they are not valuable. If measurements are used to drive actions, this changes the way the organisation works and move towards a performance- and outcome-driven culture.

- Measure what you can control – avoid what you can only influence. It's important that measures are set based on what you can control at the right level of the organisation. If a target is not being reached, the team that is reviewing it needs to be able to take the appropriate action.

- Be patient – automate and integrate measures into performance management only when you have tested them. Too often, organisations want to move quickly to having their scorecards fully systematised and automated in their formalised performance management system. Only do this once you are sure you have a stable set of measures, or if you have an agile organisation that can quickly adapt systems and processes. Developing the most effective long-term measures can take time.

Focus on outcomes, not process

CASE STUDY – A MEASUREMENT FRAMEWORK TO COMPLEMENT ANNUAL OBJECTIVES

The global team we first met in Chapter 2 when they developed annual objectives together also developed a complementary measurement framework. When they planned for the following year, they used this framework to think about what outcomes they would like to see, rather than the activities they thought were needed. This enabled more creativity in how they could achieve the outcomes, better collaboration and more stretching targets.

It's often easy when you start to move towards a vision and implement some actions to identify completed milestones as the only signs of progress. This is not always useful as you can hide true progress behind process updates that give a false impression that there has been movement. It is important to do work that builds the foundation for the future, but the more important question is what impact it has made on reaching your vision. To know this, you need to have business goals that are measurable.

Monitor and evaluate

If you and your team have agreed and defined measurements, it is critical you take action, otherwise you are wasting time. Each measure owner is responsible for identifying reasons why results are not achieving their targets, and then creating actions to address this.

This brings up potential challenges:

- Are the measures at the right level? That is, can the group who are reviewing the measure take actions that will move results to meet the target? Are those who are doing the work making decisions rather than those who are overseeing it? If there is a group of people who can make a change without referring it to others, then they should be the ones making decisions.

- If measures are being reviewed by a group, be clear about the purpose of the review. You may want to celebrate and recognise success if measures are on target. You may need to ask for support/resources to enact solutions. You may want to brainstorm solutions. You may need to review whether a measure is still relevant or useful. All of these are valid, but the purpose of the review and monitoring needs to be clear.

Key takeaways

- Understand the hurdles and challenges that you need to address in measuring your success.

- Enhance focus, alignment and efficiency by taking the journey to measuring success.

- Use a balanced scorecard to create long-term measures that reflect success from each stakeholder's perspective.

- Apply best practice and learning from previous experiences. Use practical tips that make measuring a valuable part of leading change.

- Ensure you measure outcomes/results rather than just looking at actions that have been completed, so you know you are making progress that is impactful.

- Take action as a result of measuring.

8

Meet Effectively

Once you have great measures in place, the next success factor in leading change is to conduct meetings that support these measures. As a leader of change, you need to be effective in the meetings you lead so that you:

- Build engagement in creating a vision for the future by involving the right stakeholders

- Enable implementation by ensuring focus and accountability

- Create value for participants in your meetings so that you deepen relationships

You have a foundation for successful meetings when you:

- Have strong capabilities in strategic thinking (Chapter 2)

- Have clarity of purpose for the team (Chapter 3)

- Have strong facilitation skills (Chapter 4)

- Are listening to the right stakeholders (Chapter 5)

- Have mechanisms that support different perspectives being heard (Chapter 6)

You can categorise leading change meetings into two types:

- Leadership workshops that create or review strategic direction (planning meetings)

- Leadership meetings that monitor implementation (implementation meetings)

This chapter describes how you can have productive, interactive meetings in both these scenarios. If you create the environment, focus on outcomes, are disciplined in planning and have agenda items that help you to achieve what is needed, you are likely to have meetings that are engaging and focused, and will achieve results.

Create a productive environment

CASE STUDY – STRUCTURE ACHIEVES GOALS

A not-for-profit organisation's board meetings were held monthly on a Monday night. The board members started with food and wine, and because they were such a friendly group, a lot of socialising took place and the meetings would run late into the evening as they tried to get some business done. They didn't structure the agenda items and often made decisions arbitrarily after long, rambling discussions. If people volunteered to be part of the board, they were automatically included to foster a sense of engagement, which added to chaos in the meetings.

Some board members got fed up. It felt like they were wasting time, which they could have spent with their family or doing their day-to-day work. When a new chair was appointed, she determined that the board meetings should become more efficient, while retaining the camaraderie of the group. With the support of a few advisors, she suggested these steps to enable the group to become more effective:

- Develop a clear overall vision for the organisation
- Agree how to measure success
- Clarify the purpose of the board and subcommittees
- Define roles for everyone on the board to leverage their strengths and time
- Structure the agendas and clarify decision-making processes
- Agree and record actions to be reviewed at the next meeting

The organisation grew and started to achieve its (now well-defined) goals. Board meetings were reduced to two hours in length and became much more efficient and effective. The board members knew what was expected of them and came prepared with recommendations for support by others, so a sense of accountability grew. Offline work in subcommittees became the new way of working.

The board built social time in at the end of the agenda, but this was optional for those who had other commitments. People were happy to volunteer to be on the board as they felt their time was respected and they understood how they could contribute.

The steps that the chair in our case study used can make your meetings more effective, too. By creating clarity for attendees about what you expect from the meeting and how they can contribute, you show them that it is a good use of their time.

Showing the link between different meetings will result in the right people being involved at each meeting. Outputs from one meeting can be inputs to another. The board in our case study used different kinds of meetings to make them effective. They ran workshops to create a vision for how the organisation would operate in the future, and this was separated from monitoring progress.

A big reason behind their success was that they designed each meeting to focus on what was needed and who needed to be there to make it successful. You can use the same principles to create effectiveness for each meeting that you lead. Running better meetings, especially in senior teams, is a big part of leading change, as the case study shows. Without the discipline of well-run meetings, you reduce your chances of meaningful change.

Focus on meeting outcomes

The board meeting case study shows how you can dramatically improve meeting efficiency by focusing on outcomes and creating a good structure. But you need to strike a balance as sometimes there can be too much structure, which makes a meeting feel bureaucratic.

CASE STUDY – A CULTURE SHIFT

Within a large pharmaceutical organisation, the culture was process heavy. The leadership team focused on how the end goal was reached rather than the goal itself. It was a difficult challenge to address as the leaders of the organisation had been successful previously by planning things out and monitoring milestones, but this way of working was not sustainable for the new business model.

Defining the critical measures that would demonstrate movement towards their vision was tough as it was a culture change in itself. The goal was to shift the regular leadership team meetings to be exclusively focused on outcome measures. If it was important, there would be a measurement associated with it; if it wasn't, then it wouldn't make it on to the agenda.

The leadership team put a framework for how to do this in place and agreed accountability to develop and implement individual measures. Their agendas were changed to focus on a scorecard, with owners reporting on results, sharing action plans and asking for support as needed.

The focus of the leaders shifted to achieving outcomes and recognising successes. The teams recommended action plans and identified any support needed from the leaders. The team process became clear and responsibility for how outcomes would be achieved was appropriately delegated to those who could action this.

As a by-product, this led to a more efficient annual planning process focused on setting targets for the scorecard.

It's easy to have implementation meetings that are structured around what you *need to talk about,* or what you *need to do.* By moving to meetings that are focused on what you *need to achieve,* you open up a more meaningful discussion that allows participants to be both creative and accountable. Like the team in the case study, tie your meetings directly to your vision and annual objectives. Your scorecard can drive meeting agendas and you can engage participants in celebrating success or gain their support to get back on track, creating a more outcome-focused meeting.

Design planning meetings where you are creating your future to be outcome focused too. Define what it is you need to achieve when you are meeting to plan the future.

Create an effective structure

CASE STUDY – PLANNING A SUCCESSFUL MEETING

A medical and scientific organisation was being challenged to ensure it had the right operating model. Different functions were being added and the outsourcing of various capabilities that was in place was being reviewed to ensure it was fit for the future direction of the organisation.

There was also an immediate issue that needed to be resolved quickly. It was a time when the organisation was in flux with many things changing, so there was a sense of urgency to take action and regain control.

The leader had booked a day with his growing team to make some decisions on how to move forward. After the facilitator had met with all the team members individually, it became apparent that each had a different perspective on what the agenda should be. The conversations they collectively thought they needed to have wouldn't all fit into a single day, so the only agreement was that the urgent issue needed to be addressed.

As this was likely to be the only chance that the global team would have to meet face to face in the calendar year, they needed to use the time wisely and strategically. The facilitator and leader developed a structured agenda so it was clear what was required and people were requested to bring the relevant information for input. They allocated time at the start of the meeting to reflect on their vision and the behaviours they had previously agreed. This enabled:

- The team to be re-grounded in their goals
- New members of the team to see the overall direction and feel part of the group
- Decisions to be taken in the context of the bigger picture

Overall, the discussions were productive and the meeting achieved more than the leader had expected within its time.

This planning meeting was successful because:

- The facilitator developed a clear structure based on what needed to be achieved (the outcomes of the meeting)
- Everyone had a chance to input
- The team took a big-picture perspective (rather than just addressing an immediate issue)
- Everyone respected that new members needed to feel part of the team
- Each agenda item had a clear process to work through and people completed pre-work to make this efficient

Do you really need a meeting structure? Some people say they prefer to have free-flowing discussions, but paradoxically, structure enables creativity. Create an agenda that contains and is structured around having a free-flowing conversation. This will give permission for people to be creative.

One of the best tools you can use to prepare for an effective meeting is from Lean Sigma methodology.

Known as a SIPOC (Suppliers, Inputs, Process, Outputs, Customer),[41] it was originally intended to look at any work and understand via workflows:

- What the inputs to a work process are and who supplies them

- What goes on within an activity

- What the outputs of a work process are and who the customer is

You can use the IPO part of a SIPOC to create a meeting structure. Inputs are the pre-work you need to do before the meeting, process is the agenda and approach you will take, and outputs are the results or outcomes of the meeting.

Having a structure is critical when you are leading planning meetings. Not being clear about what you need from a meeting reduces your chances of successful change being planned or implemented.

The three steps you need:

- Define what outputs you need from a meeting, eg increased understanding, feeling excited about the change ahead, a decision, an action plan.

- Develop processes that will enable each of the outputs to be achieved. This could be a flip-charted discussion, a brainstorming session, a structured presentation with key decision points outlined, etc. From this, develop an agenda with timings and ownership to lead.

- Identify what inputs would help the meeting to be effective. Then request these inputs as pre-work so that participants come to meetings prepared and ready to contribute.

If you can structure your planning meetings or your implementation meetings using an IPO, then the precious time you have together with your teams will be well used. Often there are standard items in these kinds of meetings so you only need to define inputs, process and outputs once.

Include standard items

Any planning meeting needs to be designed depending on what you require as outputs (Chapter 3), but there are some items to consider for every meeting.

Welcome, objectives, context

- Make sure that everyone knows each other.

- Explain the purpose of the meeting and the outputs you expect to get everyone focused on the meeting. Often people come into a meeting with other priorities on their minds, whether they're personal or work related, so they appreciate a few minutes to gather their thoughts and focus on why this meeting is worthy of their attention.

- Describe the context of the meeting with respect to a bigger picture. This is important because you:

  - Continue to build strategic thinking

  - May need to change your whole agenda if the context has changed dramatically since your last meeting

  - Need to reinforce the value of having a meeting. Another way to do this is to consider having a sponsor or more senior leader to kick off a meeting. This has the added benefit of getting that leader bought into the work of the team

None of this need take a long time, but this context at the start of a meeting can mean the difference between you having participants who are focused and engaged and attendees whose minds are elsewhere.

Behaviours

Developing or refreshing behaviours that ensure the success of a meeting is another critical agenda item. In Chapter 6, we discussed the importance of agreeing behaviours. It is remarkable how a reminder of what you expect can be so powerful in your meetings.

You need some creativity in how you accomplish this as you continue to repeat this agenda item, for example by asking different questions like: 'What behaviours do we need to exhibit to be successful today?' or 'How will you show up as an individual today?' Once teams have discussed behaviours a few times, all they'll need is a reminder in front of them to make it effective.

This review of behaviours is especially helpful for new members who come to a meeting. They are likely to be pleasantly surprised by the explicit commitment to sticking to an agenda (and then seeing it lived out).

Recognising success

There is a natural tendency in change-based meetings to be constantly looking forward to the next milestone and discussing what needs to be addressed. Creating time to reflect on what has gone well not only makes everyone feel good, but also builds confidence that they can address upcoming obstacles or meet milestones. One good way of doing this is to map your successes since last time you met against your vision. This continues to reinforce focus on your end goal.

Next steps/actions

Agree and be clear about what is going to happen as a next step once the meeting is complete. This can make the difference between a meeting being a waste of time or being valuable. At a minimum, clarify the next step and agree who will action it, and ideally have a timeline for each action.

Even if you have no other documented outputs, have an action register. Review actions at the next meeting to maintain visibility and accountability – this is critical for progress. And yes, this has to happen at planning meetings, otherwise great ideas are in danger of being lost.

Review/reflections

While this is one element that is not critical for individual meeting success, growing the capability of your team in collaborating with others is important for ongoing success. Take the time to reflect on what worked and didn't work in the meeting. It will lead to insights that will bring the team further together and improve future meetings. In turn, this leads to increasing the organisational capability of running more effective meetings.

One framework for doing this is an After-Action Review (AAR),[42] which is a tool that was first used by the military, and then adopted in the business world to evaluate projects. It can also be applied in meetings.

Another is the stop, start, continue framework.[43] Ask these questions:

- What should we stop doing?

- What should we start doing?

- What should we continue doing?

- What should we do less of?

- What should we do more of?

This enables you to continuously improve your meetings.

Use great meeting tools

There are many different tools and techniques you can use in meetings. Select the best one to help you to achieve your desired outcomes and outputs. Sometimes it's about creating more ideas (divergent thinking) and sometimes it's about bringing a group back into focus (convergent thinking). In most meetings, you need both kinds of thinking for success, and so different tools are helpful.

These are some tools and approaches that you may want to consider using regularly:

Sticky notes

Chapter 5 described the value of sticky notes to capture everyone's ideas, including those of team members who are quieter and more reflective than their peers. Use sticky notes at different times in the meeting, eg in developing behaviours or in the reflection process to make a meeting more engaging and to collect individuals and group insights. Summarise the ideas you gather and discuss them to come to an agreement. Group sticky notes and assign a title to each group. An electronic tool like vWall[44] can do this and is especially useful if you are running a virtual meeting.

Polling

Polling the group can dramatically cut down on the time you need to create priorities, but asking them what they think are the important ideas / issues or priorities for action can be a lengthy process. One simple way of getting to a conclusion is to give people three sticky dots that they can use as votes to prioritise a list of ideas, but it's important to check that the priorities that come out make sense for people and refine them as needed, providing further clarity. Use vWall as a digital solution in face-to-face or virtual meetings to achieve the same result. Zoom can also be used to do this virtually.

Small group work

If you have meetings that go on for longer than a few hours and involve more than ten people, it's worth considering if you can achieve more through subgroup discussions, then coming back together to share. This will increase engagement and speed up action, but extensive feedback to the larger group can seem repetitive and reduce impact, so you need to manage it. Electronic tools like Zoom have break-out rooms that can replicate this concept in virtual meetings.

Use technology effectively

Traditional skills for a modern world

In 2020, we experienced a global pandemic. Like many others, I had to work from home 100% of my time. As a meeting facilitator, I knew I had to improve my skills in conducting online meetings.

I attended webinars and looked for opportunities to practise my newfound skills. It was important that I became proficient, but what quickly struck me was that the strengths I had in facilitating meetings face to face continued to be important. If anything, for online meetings it was even more important to:

- Have a clearly defined purpose for the meeting
- Provide context and introduce others
- Agree the behaviours we were going to adopt
- Have agreed action items
- Have breaks
- Show enthusiasm
- Monitor others' engagement

Technology became a more effective way of working because I:

- Saw more people via video rather than on phone calls, which increased my connection with them
- Saved time in travel, so increased productivity
- Became more flexible in managing my day
- Enabled many different ways of getting input easily, using chat, question and answer functions, breakout rooms and vWall
- Partnered with others to have more productive meetings
- Reached out to people across the world in the same way as I did for local people

The skills that I had built over the years were as important as they had ever been. Using new tools had enhanced them.

Use your strengths in running meetings, whether they be live or virtual, and the facilitator skills we discussed in Chapter 4. Technology creates opportunities to have more effective meetings, either by including others you wouldn't normally consider because of geography, or by gathering input efficiently.

Key takeaways

- Create an environment to have great meetings. Be disciplined and use established meeting techniques, and take the time to build the groundwork for strong teamwork. Great meetings are the foundation for successful change.

- Be clear about the purpose of each meeting you lead.

- Link meetings together and have the right participants at each meeting so you are efficient and respectful of people's time.

- Focus on meeting outcomes and design the agenda and pre-work you need accordingly.

- Use a scorecard as a backbone for your implementation meetings.

- Have standard agenda items in meetings, like setting the context, agreeing behaviours, celebrating successes and reviewing effectiveness.

- Use different meeting tools to engage participants and use time wisely.

- Use technology to create a different meeting experience.

9
Implement Flawlessly

Once you have the other success factors for leading change in place, the next step of seeing your goals realised should be easy. However, many studies[45] have shown that this isn't the case because:

- The skills needed for implementation are different to creating and developing ideas

- It takes discipline and a relentless focus on the end results *and* the people who are involved in the change

- It is different for every change you lead

The importance of implementation cannot be over-emphasised and your role as a leader of change is critical. If I had to prioritise one success factor in the eight that must be done well, this would be the one.

Although each situation in implementation is different, there are commonalities that you can learn from. We have already discussed some of the key success factors that build the foundation for implementation. By choosing how to change (Chapter 3) and involving people effectively in planning (Chapter 5), you have created momentum for change that is not overwhelming. By having clear success measures (Chapter 7), you have clarified what needs to change. Having effective meetings (Chapter 8) will create a culture of focus and alignment.

In this chapter, we will look at additional aspects of implementation which will help you to embed change in your organisation flawlessly:

- Think of the big picture to put change into context.

- Prioritise, focus and manage change overload to ensure that you are not overwhelmed.

- Apply project management tools to ensure progress is being made and tasks are being done.

- Create accountability so everyone knows what they are expected to do.

- Use change-management skills to involve your stakeholders and focus on the people side of change.

- Recognise and reinforce success so that the organisation is ready for the next wave of change, with teams feeling confident they can address it based on their successes to date.

- Follow up relentlessly.

You as a change leader have a role to ensure your organisation has the capability to implement flawlessly.

Think of the big picture

Some senior leaders say that once they have defined their goals, then it is up to the rest of the organisation to implement them. Unfortunately, this is only true if these conditions are in place:

- People responsible for implementation have the authority to make decisions and the information they need to course correct.

- There is a stable external and internal environment, so expectations of outcomes don't change.

- The implementation team has the ability to think strategically (long term and broadly).

- Any barriers that exist in implementation can be addressed.

- The motivation to get to results is strong.

This is why leaders of change have a critical role in implementation. As external changes continue to accelerate, you will need to find time to reflect so you can recoalesce and realign internal priorities. You will need to reset expectations and communicate effectively, especially across departments.

Prioritise and focus

Prioritising and focusing, continuing to monitor organisational overload and progress towards objectives, remain key roles for change leaders.

CASE STUDY – BIG PICTURE OVERVIEW LEADS TO EMPLOYEE SATISFACTION

It was two years post-merger of a large organisation and the teams were stressed from the many waves of change that had hit them. New information systems, new benefits packages and new ways of working had been put in place rapidly, and employee satisfaction was dipping. The executive leadership team decided they needed a better way of managing change.

A baseline survey that described how change was typically implemented identified areas for improvement. For the first time, the leadership team created an inventory of all proposed cross-functional projects, including impact, resources needed and benefits. A steering committee was set up with the purpose of recommending to the executive team if and when projects should be implemented.

Synergies between proposed projects led to more efficient implementation, and best practices from change and project management were shared when the steering committee met. This increased cross-functional awareness at the executive team level and contributed to organisational focus. Through this process, the number of projects and the amount of 'change fatigue' were also reduced, leading to increased employee satisfaction.

This example shows the benefit of having a big-picture perspective and an overview of all the projects that are going on. In Chapter 1, we defined strategic initiatives as the three to five big initiatives that will address your organisation's key issues and get you to your vision. A strategic initiative will be a project or a group of projects. You may also have projects that are more operational or shorter term in nature, so you could have many projects going on in your organisation.

Many organisations now have a portfolio manage-ment approach to oversee and implement different projects. This enables you to allocate resources more effectively as it increases the visibility of people who are assigned to projects and helps to reduce organ-isational stress. The added dimension described in the case study, looking at each project's impact on individuals, can be of huge benefit to teams. This is especially true in larger organisations for first-line managers, who can easily be overwhelmed when change appears to be coming in all directions.

In times of significant change, it may seem that taking resources away from doing work to prioritise and focus is not responsive or agile. Of course, this is not usually true. During these periods, it is even more important for you to reassess the risks and benefits of each project or strategic initiative so that you can focus on what is important given the current situation. It is also a good time to re-examine the costs of projects, as often you need additional resources to respond to change.

What are you are not going to do?

This question always seems to be a challenge for organisations, and I have seen many leaders avoid it because they want to see all their ideas implemented. They selected projects because they were important, and once they've invested time in these projects, it is hard to give any of them up.

This is understandable, but not helpful to an over-loaded organisation. In this scenario, resources are diluted and people are left doing many different activities, making slow progress on each. The projects/tasks that get done are typically the ones that seem simple, or the ones that have strong project leaders, or those that a leader has made their individual (rather than organisational) priority. Or the organisation continues to do what it has always done as day-to-day work consumes resources rather than people finding time for what is critical, but sometimes less urgent: to move the organisation forward. Sound familiar?

You need to prioritise at an organisational, team and individual level (and ensure alignment). Prioritisation requires transparency in communication and strong influencing capabilities to persuade others that the organisation no longer needs certain activities and projects.

With solid clarity of priorities and your role, effective self-management and good, open questioning which ensures you're fully informed of the latest context, you as a leader are likely to be more self-assured. You will be more in charge of your choices, enabling you to articulate your priorities with integrity and a generosity of spirit, even if you are, in the end, saying no. If all individuals in an organisation increase their ability to effectively say no, organisational performance will rise to a new level.

Here is a step-by-step guide to help you to prioritise.

Actively select and implement priorities

Selecting the three to five top strategic initiatives, as defined in Chapter 1, that will move the organisation forward is a great first step. Name them with strong language like 'Strategic Imperatives' or 'Battles to be Won' or 'Big Rocks' to capture attention and aid focus.

These initiatives are the important few that will make the organisation if you address them effectively, or break it if you do not.

What is the one thing (the 'home run') that you absolutely need to achieve? Make sure everyone knows that all other priorities are secondary, creating clear focus and enabling better decision making. Communicate that people should not work on other projects.

Clarify roles and be conscious of overload

In a world where roles are constantly changing, matrix (cross-functional) working is becoming the norm, as is an expectation that we will all be proactive and collaborative. Not surprisingly, roles are becoming more diffuse and lacking in clarity. As a change leader, you need to constantly clarify your role (as an individual or as a team) to focus on delivering the most value and not get overloaded by additional tasks. You will have times when you do take on extra work, but being aware of this, and ensuring the work is temporary, is the first step to managing workload.

Identify low-priority activities that you can abandon

Have an active and visible goal to abandon low-priority activities, and create mechanisms to achieve this. This is often forgotten by leaders. Giving people the right to say no will reduce perception of overload and allow them to focus on organisational imperatives rather than feeling stressed.

Hold meetings where abandonment is the focus. List all the activities that are being done and ask, 'What can we take off our plate?' Understand the associated risks and any barriers that would stop you moving forward so that everyone feels comfortable abandoning activities/projects when they leave the meeting.

When you're searching for abandonment ideas, capture opportunities to reduce workload by asking, 'What can be delayed to another day?' or 'What task can be reduced or diminished?' which will help to focus your organisation on those activities that are truly important. By identifying and communicating activities you have abandoned, you are sharing the importance of prioritising so that you can focus on success.

Identify the behaviours that are stopping you saying no

Despite setting priorities, clear roles and mechanisms to help you focus, you may sometimes find it's still hard to say no. It might be that you have a tendency to micromanage, or you're hyper competitive, or a bit of a pleaser. All of these traits can mean you do more than is yours to do, leading to resentment, friction and demotivation in both you and others. Meanwhile, efficiency decreases, alongside a rise in task duplication within the business.

Many people are concerned that saying no will create tension, conflict and come across as unhelpful, flying in the face of the typically expected can-do attitude. A great option is to ask solid questions that help everyone to understand changing priorities, for example, 'This sounds like a new priority. Is that right?' or 'How does this sit alongside the previous priorities we've agreed?' or 'What needs to stop for this new activity to take priority?'

Prioritisation needs to be learned and practised.

Apply project management tools

You make a promise, whether it's as a child at school or in business today, and you have to keep it. When you say you will do something by a certain time, delivering on that expectation is a basic requirement, especially in business.

Why is it difficult to keep your promises? Your challenge in the workplace is that it takes many stakeholders with many competing priorities and different skills to work together seamlessly to achieve a large goal. Project management is essential.

I define project management very simply as coordinating and delivering the tasks that need to be done to achieve an outcome on time and within budget. Project management has its roots in construction and other industries where it is critical to specify and deliver on time. In those industries, the discipline is well established, and there are many great courses and certifications to help you build this skill to a finely tuned level.[46] The challenge is applying the skill in sectors where work is more fluid, and the structure and discipline that comes with strong project management is seen as over bureaucratic and not conducive to being agile.

Using basic principles of project management can greatly increase your chances of keeping your promises to your stakeholders. What is the essence of good project management that you can apply even in small, fluid organisations?

Be clear about the goal

There are many questions that will help you get clear about your project goal:

- What will the project outcome be?

- How will you measure the impact?

- What will stakeholders notice as a result?

- How will things be different as a result of the project?

- What is the tangible deliverable?

- When will the project be finished?

- What is the specific timeline you are working towards?

- Are there interim deliverables?

- Is this specific project aligned with your strategic goals?

- Do all stakeholders agree with the stated goals?

Collate this information and summarise your current state and corresponding future state using a 'from: to' table, like the example below.[47]

From: Where we are today	To: Where we will be in three years
Some successes with individual functions and partners	All critical partners will understand the complexity of what we do and their role in using organisational time wisely
Feeling of lack of respect for our time	There will be minimum rework/ last-minute requests due to not consulting us earlier
Partners don't include us in plans, which makes us work in a reactive/ unplanned way	

This helps you to assess the size of the change you are making, check overlap with other goals and manage scope, which increases focus. It allows you to set clear outcome measures of success or align them with existing measures.

Involve the right people

Some of the questions that you can use to check you are involving the right people are:

- What skillsets do you need to be part of the project to deliver on your promise?

- Will you be able to get people with these skills to work on your project?

- Are there people on the team who have done these kinds of projects before?

- Do you need resources from outside your organisation?

- Who will project manage?

- Do you need a change manager?

- Do you need communication specialists?

- Do human resources (HR), finance or information technology (IT) specialists need to be involved?

- Do you need to have everyone at every team meeting, or is having access to time as needed more efficient?

- Will people be motivated to contribute their best?

- How will you continue to motivate them?

- Who will sponsor the project?

Each major strategic initiative needs to be owned by a project manager who will develop an action plan that has clear resources, needs and timelines. The action plan should be developed with representation from people who are impacted across the organisation.

Identify who will sponsor each initiative. Their role will be to provide resources and have a big-picture perspective, communicate and build support for the project across the organisation. Typically, the sponsor will have been involved in identifying why the initiative is important and will be personally motivated to make sure it succeeds.

Create an action plan

Once you have the right people on your team, you can create an action plan together by asking these questions:

- What are the key deliverables within the project?

- What needs to get done to reach your goal? When do these tasks need to be achieved?

- What tasks are dependent on others?

- What is the critical path you need to follow to get to the goal effectively?

- What tasks will trigger others?

- What tasks can be done in parallel?

- What could happen that could derail the project?

- How could you build in tasks that would help to mitigate these risks?

You need to take other priorities into account so that you can agree realistic timelines. Considering the timing and interactive nature of the tasks will help you to order activities and manage expectations. Assume that implementing each initiative will take 25–50% more time than you think (consider your track record and how unexpected priorities divert you from longer-term initiatives).

Make the action plan visible to everyone involved, either through manual systems or team-shared areas, to drive clarity and set expectations. Ensure there is good communication between the sponsor and project manager to confirm the scope of the project.

Define the cost

It's important that you understand how much you are investing in a specific initiative and set up systems to track this investment. Once you've defined the activities, you can get a better estimate of:

- How much the project will cost

- How much time you will need from each of your team members

- Other resources you will need

These can be difficult to assess. Skilled people like IT and finance professionals are invaluable as you make decisions on whether to progress.

Once you have estimates, put them into budgets and your finance systems so they can be tracked. Don't let your financial budgeting systems and timings drive business decisions rather than business needs driving budgets.

Track results

This is the most critical part of project management. You can:

- Use tracking sheets that describe progress and are shared with team members and sponsors alike to increase the visibility and create accountability

- Review action registers and follow up between each meeting

- Use a measurement scorecard that shows the results (impact) of your project

As a project sponsor or leader of change, your role is to make sure tracking is being done rather than taking over from your project manager. Take the time to set expectations on when and how you will get updates.

Develop communication plans

Communicate project goals in the context of other initiatives and explain why they are important to ensure that everyone is working on priorities. Your project managers need to have a communication plan that has addressed these questions:

- Is people's work going to change as a result of this project?

- Who will need to be updated on project progress?

- When and how will you communicate to your stakeholders?

Communication is critical throughout the project. Projects will change as you progress (especially for less concrete ones), either in what they deliver or how much it will cost. You need to share this.

Create accountability

CASE STUDY – R&D LEADERS OWN THEIR BUSINESS PLANS

Post-merger, the target set for investment seemed unlikely to be met by an R&D organisation. It was not clear what the teams needed to do to meet the target or what the appropriate target contribution for each department should be.

The departmental leaders had strong scientific expertise. They understood why they needed to meet this target, so they created a business plan template to show how each R&D department could grow its areas and contribute to achieving the overall target. This included investment targets, customer relationship strategies and resource projections. Each department leader was accountable to complete the templates with support from business planners and finance, and then present to each other to allow for challenge and support of their plan. This was a different way of working to that which the departments had been used to.

As the process repeated each year, the next layer of managers became more involved, increasing the business acumen and strategic thinking capability of the division. Each of the leaders dramatically improved their understanding of the business of the other departments. They used plans to communicate to stakeholders and investors. Most importantly, they achieved the R&D investment target.

This example shows how you can create accountability by setting expectations and sharing the results. If you provide tools and support to the leaders, they will be able to contribute effectively to success.

How many times have you been in meetings with people you thought were accountable to deliver tasks, only to find that was not what they believed? It is particularly frustrating when these people report to you.

When you're a leader of cross-functional projects, the challenge becomes even larger and the skill of creating accountability more critical. If people don't feel accountable, then tasks or projects won't get done, but one of the biggest challenges within teams (and organisations) is creating a culture where people feel personally accountable.

There can be many reasons why lack of accountability happens, but they can be summarised in two ways:

- Don't want to – people haven't bought into the task as they don't see the value for themselves or the organisation in completing the work. Have you created the environment where people have the chance to articulate for themselves why projects or tasks are important, as we discussed in Chapter 5?

- Not able to – what people are being asked to do isn't clear, they believe they don't have the skills to complete it successfully, they haven't been given permission to do it, or they don't have the time to do.

Sometimes these two basic reasons are combined. People appear not to want to do the task because they don't believe it is a priority over the myriad of other tasks they have on their plate. This is why the organisational ability to prioritise is so important.

Often people will revert to the activities that they have always done, especially if they don't understand why they need to change or know how they can contribute to achieving the organisational goals. In larger organisations, this means you will need to be a strong communicator. You will need to create a forum where everyone can discuss the bigger picture and the changes that are going on in the environment, review organisational priorities and agree clear expectations. If each person in the organisation has contributed to organisational priorities and taken ownership in setting their own personal goals in line with these, they will have a bigger commitment to executing these goals.

A useful model to create accountability was devised by Roger Connors and Tom Smith.[48] A four-step process of form, communicate, align and inspect expectations, it allows for any misalignment on clarity, skills and priorities to become clear, and you can use it whether you are a leader of a team, influencing others, a project or change manager who is creating accountability for a cross-functional team where there is no formal authority, or a line manager.

Top tips to create accountability:

- Start by discussing why the project and the individual goals are important.

- Ensure that the accountability environment has been set up. Will successful completion of the tasks reflect well on the individuals involved? Will individuals be recognised (in the way they like to be) for their contribution by their managers?

- Make sure you have clarified expectations and are checking understanding. Use the Connors and Smith four-step process of form, communicate, align and inspect expectations.

- Never leave a (project) meeting without clear next steps. Ideally, write them down so they are visible on a screen or flip chart with people's names and due date. Discuss and negotiate due dates so you are comfortable that people are fully clear and committing. If you assign actions to people outside the room, ensure someone in the room is accountable to let them know and make sure they understand.

- Make accountability transparent. Share reports of who has completed tasks that have been agreed and who has not. This really encourages completion before the next meeting. Stay neutral and non-confrontational for this to work well.

- Close the loop – discuss why accountability is not happening. Start each project meeting reviewing whether actions have been done or not, as described in Chapter 8. Taking the next step of delving into why actions have not been completed can move you closer towards a culture of accountability within your team.

If you are finding problems with people taking on accountability in cross-functional teams where you are leading peers or reports of peers, then engage them as we discussed in Chapter 5.

Use change-management skills

CASE STUDY – BUILD CHANGE MANAGEMENT CAPABILITY

In Chapter 1, we looked at a case study of a global manufacturer that had used various change-management tools to make its implementation of a new automation system successful. The same group of leaders decided they needed some dedicated change-management resources for the project. Instead of having a single professional change-management resource, they identified representatives from each of the organisation's three pilot sites. Each representative knew the culture of their site but was not a full-time change manager. Instead, they were coached by an outside expert.

They:

- Created stakeholder maps for the three pilot sites
- Collected successes and learnings from previous changes
- Developed sponsor contracts so those leading the change knew what was expected of them
- Developed change, communications and training plans

- Organised training in change management for key members of the project team

They then facilitated a series of workshops to:

- Kick off project teams
- Assess the impact of change
- Engage business sponsors
- Further develop communication and training plans

This led to a shift in business readiness for the system implementation with stakeholders embracing the benefits that the system brought. Having effective change management capability was critical.

This case study shows how you can maximise internal business knowledge with external expertise to grow capability to manage change effectively in the future. The organisation in the case study used many different tools based on what was needed. You too can select the right approach for your situation by having a strong change-management toolkit.

The change-management skills that the large project in the case study used were a combination of specialist change managers and people who knew the subject matter. Have people who specialise in projects and change to bring the discipline and neutrality you need. Also, ensure you have people who understand the culture of the organisation. You may find these skills in the same person, or the in-depth skills described in the case study may not be necessary for smaller, less impactful changes. Each situation is different.

Communicate success

In Chapter 1, we defined the importance of communication. Creating and delivering a good communication plan is a key element of implementation. This section describes some top tips for effective communication as a leader of change.

Sometimes change is positive, but often we have to communicate negative consequences, and the reality is no one wants to be the bearer of bad news. As a leader of change, how do you remain honest and transparent while acting with empathy and integrity?

- Describe *why* change is being made. Link back to overall organisational goals and share external environmental trends that have made this change necessary. Sometimes it's about mitigating risk and negative press attention as well as managing brand reputation.

- Be clear about *why* you (and others) have to communicate the bad news so that it's positioned with as much forethought, care and understanding as possible.

- Be clear about *what* the change is. Have a vision and purpose for the change. What are you looking for individuals to do as a result? How can they contribute to decisions about implementation? What, if anything, can be negotiated?

- Describe timelines associated with the change and *when* the next steps will happen.

- Consider *when* you'll have discussions. Don't deliver news that is hard to hear and then be slow in delivery, as this can feel even more painful. You will also need to be patient and acknowledge that there may be a period of discomfort to live through, and that individuals will be different in the way that they respond and move along the change curve.

- Consider *how* you will communicate news. Small team or individual face-to-face meetings allow for feedback and assessing reactions. You often need the whole mix of online, social and print options to reinforce the change strategy following face-to-face discussions.

- Consider *who* is going to lead discussions. People like to hear overall direction and goals from their senior leaders, and this is critical for strong engagement, but individuals want to discuss the specific impact for them with their direct managers. Everyone approaches change from an individual survival perspective – the 'What's in it for me?' – so make your communications outcome oriented and tailored to the individual(s)/ audience.

- Be honest and acknowledge the extent of the negative impact(s). Share *how* you are planning to mitigate negative consequences. What support will be in place, eg opportunity to discuss the change further / feedback channels?

- Reinforce the positive (from your recipient's perspective) aspects of the change. Actively ask for support and input to enable the positive outcomes to be realised.

- Listen. Check for understanding. Continue to communicate. You will need to repeat the same message many times; don't assume that because you have said things once, people have absorbed and understood them. Ensure that there is follow-up so you can hear and manage each individual's concerns. Create a feedback loop. If you are part of a broader organisational change, ensure that you are checking in with your peers about any concerns that they are hearing and addressing them in a consistent manner across the organisation.

- Consider how you will communicate with external stakeholders. Customers and suppliers may well be impacted by your decisions, or they may hear about the changes from employees rather than officially from you.

Recognise success

Just doing it!

One of the most challenging roles I had was during a reorganisation that involved the ways of working in a division of over 200 people. Resources were tight, there had been a shift to focus on customer-facing roles and the organisation needed to reduce operations/ infrastructure resources.

We focused resources on three key areas:

- Having a strong manager network
- Being able to measure benefits (savings)
- Strong communications and ability to collect innovations

After the teams were trained to run projects, we also collected, communicated and rewarded successes through a 'just doing it' programme. We set departmental goals and integrated them into performance management systems. This resulted in an emerging culture of continuous improvement, where target savings were set and achieved.

There are two learnings about recognition in this example. Firstly, you can make significant change when it's tied to compensation. Secondly, and more surprisingly at the time, you can make savings by using informal recognition routes. In the personal story example above, these included being noticed by peers for suggesting a great idea, thank yous from senior managers and prizes for good ideas.

People like to be recognised in different ways, and as a leader of change, you need to tailor your recognition to what works best for individuals. Critically, you also need to ensure your recognition reinforces what you want to change. In the example, this was a culture of continuous improvement.

CASE STUDY – BUILDING ON SUCCESS

Every year, a team met to refresh the plans they had made and to plan for the future. A critical part of this meeting was to note the progress they had made by writing down what they had done and how it contributed to moving towards their vision. They also identified what strengths they had used as individuals and as a group to achieve these results.

This had several benefits. Each member of the team:

- Recognised and felt good about progress
- Understood how their strengths had contributed to success
- Felt rejuvenated and ready to do more in the upcoming year
- Felt confident that they could continue to accomplish because of what they had already achieved
- Embedded new ways of working

By recognising the progress they had made on a regular basis, the team kept themselves focused and aligned on their vision.

Recognising success with your team and focusing on how it links to your vision is critical for leaders of change. It demonstrates the importance of achieving your vision and the criticality of team performance.

This reinforces the ways of working you have set up and builds a strong platform for future success.

Follow up relentlessly

The key to successful implementation ultimately comes down to follow-up. Relentless follow-up is critical to ensure forward movement.

This can take many forms. You can:

- Measure outcomes to ensure your teams are making an impact (Chapter 6)

- Have effective meetings to check in on progress (Chapter 8)

- Use project management tools (see earlier in this chapter)

- Hold people accountable (see earlier in this chapter)

The desire and skill to continue to follow up until a task is complete is invaluable. Use formal check-ins to hold accountability and reconfirm priorities. Adjust priorities based on changes in the environment and reset accountabilities if need be. Remember if you are a sponsor, your role is to create the expectation that this follow-up will happen and not jump into being a project manager yourself.

Key takeaways

- Recognise as a leader that you have a critical role in implementation. Think about the big picture and how the environment will impact the work that is being done.

- Have a portfolio management approach to change to enable you to look at the total impact on the organisation and manage change overload.

- Decide your priorities and communicate them. Be clear about individuals' roles in achieving priorities. Learn how to say no gracefully.

- Use simple project management tools to ensure your implementation stays on track. Have clear goals, the right people in place, agreed action plans, defined costs, tracking mechanisms, communication and change plans.

- Create an environment where taking accountability is easy. Recognise that taking accountability for actions can be tough because people either don't want to or aren't able to due to other priorities.

- Use specialised change-management skills when initiatives will significantly impact the way people work. Look internally and externally to build capability for projects and the future.

- Recognise results and desired behaviours to embed change. Different people like to be recognised in different ways.

- Recognise results and strengths to reenergise a team to take on new work.

- Follow up relentlessly to ensure implementation happens.

10

Create Effective Change Leadership For Future Success

We have discussed the eight important success factors to prepare for, lead and implement change flawlessly. This final chapter summarises the skills you need as a change leader. It describes the value of internal and external consulting support and how to choose the right partner, and the rewards you will see as a result of great change leadership.

How I help teams increase strategic thinking

The fact that my career has been about increasing strategic thinking was a recent insight. I thought what I was doing was helping teams and individuals develop and deliver long-term plans so they could succeed. While this is true, it's more than that.

One day, someone asked me, 'Can you help our managers think more strategically?'

'I'm not a trainer,' I said. 'I don't develop people; I facilitate them through a process.' Then I thought about some of the great teams I have worked with and realised that they grew their strategic thinking capability by:

- Doing the work in creating plans
- Implementing those plans
- Reviewing and updating on a regular basis

They've expanded their time horizons from annual plans to five-year plans. They have broadened their thinking, not just in terms of their team and the immediate environment, but also by considering a range of stakeholders who are impacted by the decisions they make. They are amazing strategic thinkers.

Incidentally, their organisations have also benefited in many ways and achieved remarkable results – whether it be measured in market share, revenue, profitability, or by a more intangible value, for example employee engagement or customer satisfaction.

Seeing strategic thinking in action and participating in strategic planning increases your individual and organisational capability to lead change. Learning through training gives you basic frameworks and models, but if you're not working alongside others who challenge you and your approach, you can underestimate the multidimensional nature of change. A default to basic step-by-step processes is inefficient and frustrating.

Leverage the capabilities you need

The capabilities that a change leader needs for success include those that I described through my career experiences in the Introduction:

- Structured systems thinking – the ability to think from a customer perspective and translate that into what the organisation needs to do. You understand that the organisation is about meeting customer needs and there is a series of processes that lead to doing so. You know that these processes are by their nature cross-functional so that interactions between functions become critical for success. You apply process improvement tools and techniques to create effective change.

- Cross-functional thinking – the ability to think across organisations and reach over functional barriers. You can impact people's behaviour without having a reporting relationship, establish impact without formal control, integrate organisation-wide thinking and focus on overarching organisational goals.

- Bringing value – the ability to understand what success looks like and how to achieve results. You move initiatives by understanding what works across the organisation, knowing that success and results can be multidimensional and different stakeholders can see them differently, and that all needs have to be met. This enables you to understand the intricacies of how each activity is important to drive results.

- Strategic thinking – the ability to think ahead and across organisational barriers. You turn long-term thinking into deliverable goals, have a big-picture perspective and the ability to drill down to the next level to understand how conceptual ideas can be made tangible, and combine cross-functional thinking with bringing value to get results.

- Partnership consulting – the ability to understand ambiguous organisational challenges and resolve them through an optimal approach. You recognise that one size does not fit all, have a toolkit that can understand the challenges of an organisation and bring the most appropriate solution without unnecessary process overload.

As a leader of change, you don't have to have all these capabilities yourself. Look to your peers and teams who have complementary capabilities and skills, or look externally. Having an external partner who brings these skillsets and provides a neutral mindset has its own value (see Chapter 4).

Internal consulting support

Once you decide that it would be useful to have some support to help you to lead change, look within your organisation, especially if you are part of a large organisation that has this kind of internal resource.

Internal consulting groups can build an extensive knowledge of the business and its language/jargon. They bring a consistent approach to change in all its forms with a methodology and language that you can use. In turn, you can grow change capability more easily throughout the organisation. Internal consulting groups have more objectivity than leaders who have functional, people and cost-centre accountabilities. They can be used to guide others along the change path.

Sometimes, internal change consultants are not as valued as external consultants. There is an illogical perception that they are not being paid for their skills, as the visibility of the payment is not transparent, so they are seen as a luxury if there are no major change projects. It is true, though, that having employees with this special expertise is not as flexible as bringing in external resources for specific projects.

For smaller organisations, dedicated internal consultants are not usually cost effective. When a consultant is embedding change expertise within operations roles, the expertise can be diluted if the consultant gets pulled into day-to-day operations, so you may choose to look to your external network as the flexibility of an external consultant who works with many organisations can be both efficient and valuable. They don't get involved with the many corporate activities that internal consultants do. Instead, they bring objectivity and best practice as an external consultant.

Choose external resource carefully

An external consultant must work with the internal organisational culture

As an internal consultant working with external consulting teams, I saw the importance of consultants working with the culture rather than imposing their own. I remember when my team and I were realigning our division to focus more on our local customers and less on global issues. This required a significant shift of mindset, and as a leadership team, we decided that it would be good to get some external help.

Our first group of consultants came in with some analytical tools and a step-by-step methodology that was both rigorous and demanding. It was too much for people who were trying to understand the new change and deliver on their day-to-day business, so we had to stop and work out how we could use what the consultants had done, but in a way that would enable rather than force the change.

Our second group of consultants were all about co-creation, working with us to integrate the reasons for the change and creating the key steps to get to where we needed to be, including engagement of our managers and employees.

It's important when you are hiring external consultants to ensure you have a good fit. In this example, each set of consultants brought a different skillset, but the first group didn't gauge the mood and culture of the organisation and tried to impose a standard methodology that didn't work for the experienced team. The second recognised the internal expertise and partnered effectively to bring exactly what we needed.

If you decide you need an external resource to provide you with a neutral objective view to complement the internal skillset that you and others have and to coach you through significant change, what should you look for? There are two factors that are critical: the right skillset and the right fit, which is a combination of background experience and chemistry. When you are leading change, you need a resource that can blend in easily with you and your organisation. As my personal story above shows, the right chemistry is key to successes.

Here are some factors to consider when you're looking for a partner to work alongside you in leading change.

Organisation and change-management expertise

You need someone who has led change and partnered with different organisations to help them deliver change. This expertise can be gained through change-management accreditations like Prosci[49] or Change Management Institute (CMI),[50] or through business courses where change management is increasingly a critical part of the curriculum. These qualifications form a strong foundation for being able to deliver change programmes. The experience of going through change programmes and using different methodologies and tools enables professionals to pick what is right for you.

A pragmatic and flexible approach that works

Look for success stories when challenging situations have arisen and an expert has used an approach that didn't create extra work above what was needed, but which worked for the situation. This flexibility to do what is needed and not use a favourite tool if it is not appropriate is important.

Experience in aligning organisations

Alignment and building on what an organisation has already done is important for three reasons:

- The momentum generated in heading in a certain direction needs to be maintained. Different directions and terminology often lead to stress and confusion. Make sure your consultants reinforce the reasons why you have started on a journey that have been internalised by employees.

- Building on a foundation acknowledges the work that people have done rather than negating or confusing those efforts.

- Influencing others in the organisation/team is easier as you add to a story rather than creating a new one.

Results and engagement orientation

Striking a balance between how people are engaged and how results will be achieved is critical. The two parts are not exclusive. For example, the traditional 'command and control' approach may seem to deliver faster implementation as leaders can decide on change, and then tell people what to do. But a more inclusive approach, which may appear to take longer to start with, leads to faster implementation and more sustained results as motivation to do the right thing increases. Look for resources that will match your desired balance.

Sector experience

A change-management skillset is transferrable across sectors, but the ability to talk the same language, interpret what a particular organisation needs and share success stories is so powerful that sector experience can make the difference in terms of speed of integration with your team and your ability to deliver results.

A track record of growing change leadership capability

As the pace of change continues to accelerate, everyone needs to increase their strategic thinking capability. It's critical to have an external resource who will come in and partner with you, and then leave behind people who have increased their strategic thinking and ability to lead change. Build in learning points through reflection and after-action reviews to enhance this capability.

A focused skillset

It's important for external resources to be clear about what they can do and what they can't. All individuals have a blend of skills, some of which are strengths and some of which are merely adequate. As a partner, you want to leverage the skills that are strengths and not use an external resource who is not uniquely qualified to lead change.

External resources who have extensive networks have a stronger sense of their unique skills, as well as the ability to call on others to do work that they are not uniquely qualified to do. These networks exist within consulting organisations and in the independent consulting community. Consultants who tap into the knowledge that these networks bring are better positioned to serve organisations more effectively.

Reap the rewards for leading change successfully

If your organisation is in the middle of change and wants to make it significant and sustainable to thrive and succeed, then using the approaches in this book could make the difference. You will be:

- Focused and aligned by ensuring you are only working on the critical goals that will really make a difference, all stakeholders understand what they are, and they are all working to achieve those same goals.

- Empowered and enabled by using co-creation in setting direction, thus allowing everyone to identify the part of the puzzle they are responsible for and feel motivated and excited about achieving it.

- Connected and partnered by reaching out to the right resources, whether they're within your organisation, your direct customers, or suppliers. Ensure that you are maximising the value for everyone in that network to engage them in your vision and use all of their talents to move towards it.

- Achieving results by partnering with your customers and suppliers and engaging your talent in efficient and effective ways of working. In this manner, you will achieve your long-term results in a sustainable way.

Leading for change is all about people creating results, whatever is going on in your environment. It is about people feeling that they are able to make the changes they see are needed because they understand the direction of the organisation and what is happening in the environment. Business today is about constantly creating and embedding change. As a leader, you need to know how to change yourself, your team and your organisation. This will enable you to create sustainable success for everyone.

Key takeaways

- Develop or leverage the unique skillsets you need for success.

- Consider what resources you can draw on internally and make an informed choice whether you need to look externally.

- Select external resources that will be effective for you. Consider change leadership capabilities and the right chemistry. Expect that skills will be transferred to your organisation.

- Reap the rewards for leading change effectively.

Notes

1. FW Taylor, *The Principles of Scientific Management* (Harper & Bros, 1911)
2. 'Definition of change management' (Prosci, n.d.), www.prosci.com/resources/articles/change-management-definition, accessed August 2020
3. H Mintzberg, B Ahlstrand and JB Lampel, *Strategy Safari: A guided tour through the wilds of strategic management* (Free Press, 1998)
4. S Sinek, *Start With Why: How great leaders inspire everyone to take action* (Portfolio, 2009)
5. 'What Is the ADKAR model?' (Prosci, n.d.), www.prosci.com/adkar/adkar-model, accessed August 2020
6. '8-step process' (Kotter, n.d.), www.kotterinc.com/8-steps-process-for-leading-change, accessed August 2020

7. www.change-management-institute.com

8. 'Executive sponsor's importance and role' (Prosci, 2018) www.prosci.com/resources/articles/importance-and-role-of-executive-sponsor, accessed August 2020

9. PM Lencioni, 'Make your values mean something', *Harvard Business Review*, 2002, https://hbr.org/2002/07/make-your-values-mean-something, accessed August 2020

10. W Aghina, A De Smet and K Weerda, 'Agility: It rhymes with stability', *McKinsey Quarterly*, 2015, www.mckinsey.com/business-functions/organization/our-insights/agility-it-rhymes-with-stability#:~:text=A%202015%20analysis%20of%20McKinsey's,on%20one%20or%20the%20other., accessed August 2020

11. GH Eoyang and RJ Holladay, *Adaptive Action: Leveraging uncertainty in your organisation* (Stanford Business Books, 2013)

12. E Kübler-Ross and D Kessler, *On Grief and Grieving: Finding the meaning of grief through the five stages of loss* (Simon & Schuster, 2005)

13. 'Executive sponsor's importance and role' (Prosci, 2018) www.prosci.com/resources/articles/importance-and-role-of-executive-sponsor, accessed August 2020

14. 'Innovation Line for Healthcare: Lets focus on the HBA case' [event], London, 2 April 2019, facilitated by Your Business Partner: www.ybusinesspartner.com

15. M Buckingham, *StandOut: The groundbreaking new strengths assessment from the leader of the strengths revolution* (Thomas Nelson, 2011)

16. J Brown and D Isaacs, *The World Café: Shaping our futures through conversations that matter* (Berrett-Koehler, 2005)

17. D Benjamin and D Komlos, *Cracking Complexity: The breakthrough formula for solving just about anything fast* (Nicholas Brearley, 2019)

18. H Mintzberg, B Ahlstrand and JB Lampel, *Strategy Safari: A guided tour through the wilds of strategic management* (Free Press, 1998)

19. DR Conner, *Managing at the Speed of Change: How resilient managers succeed and prosper where others fail* (Random House, 1993)

20. EJ Murray and PR Richardson, *Fast Forward: Organizational change in 100 days* (Oxford University Press, 2002)

21. DL Cooperrider, D Whitney and JM Stavros, *The Appreciative Inquiry Handbook: For leaders of change*, 2nd edition (Berrett-Koehler, 2008)

22. M Buckingham, *The One Thing You Need to Know:... About great managing, great leading and sustained individual success* (Simon & Schuster, 2006)

23. W Shakespeare, *The Life of Henry the Fifth*, Act 3, Scene 1. In S Wells and G Taylor (Eds) *Shakespeare: The complete works* (Book Club Associates by arrangement with Oxford University Press, 1988)

24. A Osterwalder and Y Pigneur, *Business Model Generation: A handbook for visionaries, game changers, and challengers* (John Wiley & Sons, 2010)

25. PB Marren and PJ Kennedy, 'Scenario planning for economic recovery: Short-term decision making in a recession' *Strategy and Leadership*, 38/1 (2010), pp11–16

26. www.hotspotsmovement.com

27. www.vwall.org

28. T Chamorro-Premuzic, 'Why brainstorming works better online', *Harvard Business Review*, 2015, www.hbr.org/2015/04/why-brainstorming-works-better-online, accessed August 2020

29. The Behavioural Perception Matrix, developed by Interpersonal Growth Systems Inc in 1978. Training was run by PA Carlson Communication and Training, December 1987.

30. V Hunt, D Layton, S Prince, 'Why diversity matters' (McKinsey, 2015) www.mckinsey.com/business-functions/organization/our-insights/why-diversity-matters, accessed August 2020

31. AC Edmondson, *The Fearless Organization: Creating psychological safety in the workplace for learning, innovation, and growth* (John Wiley & Sons, 2019)

32. O Kroeger, JM Thuesen and H Rutledge, *Type Talk at Work: How the 16 personality types determine your success on the job* (Bantam Doubleday Dell, 2002

33. N Herrmann and A Herrmann-Nehdi, *The Whole Brain Business Book: Unlocking the power of whole brain thinking in organizations, teams, and individuals*, 2nd edition (McGraw Hill, 2015)

34. M Scullard and D Baum, *Everything DiSC Manual* (John Wiley & Sons, 2015)

35. M Buckingham and DO Clifton, *Now, Discover Your Strengths: How to develop your talents and those of the people you manage* (Simon & Schuster, 2004)

36. PM Lencioni, *The Advantage: Why organizational health trumps everything else in business* (Jossey-Bass, 2012)

37. L Senn and J Hart, *Winning Teams – Winning Cultures* (Leadership Press, 2006)

38. K Simpson, 'Reducing the fear in networking Part 1: Preparing to network' (Upward, n.d.) www.upwardwomen.org/2018/05/22/reducing-the-fear-in-networking-part-1-preparing-to-network, accessed August 2020

39. RS Kaplan and DP Norton, 'Balanced scorecard: Measures that drive performance', *Harvard Business Review*, January–February, 1992

40. RS Kaplan and DP Norton, *Strategy Maps: Converting intangible assets into tangible outcomes* (Harvard Business Review Press, 2004)

41. PS Pande, RP Neuman and RR Cavanagh, *The Six Sigma Way: How GE, Motorola and other top companies are honing their performance* (McGraw Hill 2000)

42. M Darling, C Parry and J Moore, 'Learning in the thick of it', *Harvard Business Review*, 2005, www.hbr.org/2005/07/learning-in-the-thick-of-it, accessed August 2020

43. TJ DeLong, 'Three questions for effective feedback', *Harvard Business Review*, 2011, www.hbr.org/2011/08/three-questions-for-effective-feedback, accessed August 2020

44. www.vwall.org

45. 'Why change management' (Prosci, n.d.) www.prosci.com/resources/articles/why-change-management, accessed August 2020

46. PMI, *A Guide to the Project Management Body of Knowledge*, including 'The Standard for Project Management', www.pmi.org/pmbok-guide-standards, accessed August 2020

47. For more on gap analysis, see JP Womack and DT Jones, *Lean Thinking* (Free Press, 2003), p320.

48. R Connors and T Smith, *How Did That Happen? Holding people accountable for results the positive, principled way* (Penguin, 2009)

49. www.prosci.com

50. www.change-management-institute.com

Acknowledgements

I never dreamed five years ago that I would write a book. 'I don't write, I facilitate' was my internal message. But a few people had different ideas.

Steve Hartley, my digital marketing partner, told me I needed to blog; Hana Dickinson and Michaela Woodley invited me to contribute to their e-book; and I started to write blogs of 500 words in September 2017. Emerging from a coffee with Ket Patel in spring 2019, I realised that I had written half the content of a book through the blogs.

Thanks to my blog reviewers and co-authors: Cat Guynan, Priya Mande, Janette Thomas, Kevin Canning, Mike Mair, Marcia Mendes d'Abreu, Martino Picardo, Barbara Henders, John Ryan, Lynn Cunningham,

Mariana Viera, Julia Sullivan, Emer Wynne, Kevin Cox, Andy Chilton, John Wenger, Andy Williams, Sally Moore, Raymond Castonguay, Tony Jones, Kris Shah, Pat Goldthorpe, Susanne Mikler, Anne Gilmore, Remo Gujer, Neil Shortman. You have all done more than reviewing an article and have been significant players and thought leaders in my work life.

It was a joy to reflect on and collate work experiences, and there are many people who have been significant in my career, whether as partners, bosses, clients, coaches or colleagues. The rich experiences I have described in this book came about because you were part of them. The list includes: Kevin Pope and my colleagues at Four Square; Ann Simm; Beth Johnson; Michael Levy and his leadership team; the BSI team; my MBO team; Rav Kumar; John Dillon and his leadership teams; Glenn Crater, Joanne Kowell Anderson and Diane Drolet; Suzanne Bergeron; Suzanne Villeneuve; Janet Laughton Mackay; the CLT; the F&O team; John Pottage and CSMOLT; Alaisdar Graham and Kristin Killin; Pat Campbell; Rob Tessarolo; Bruce Clark and his leadership team; Dianne Lee and her leadership team; Sara Nixon; Sandra Cruickshanks; the Syntegrity team. A special mention to Anne Dean who has been integral to my success over the last fifteen years and was a catalyst in me writing this book.

I've been truly lucky to have Karon West in my life for over twenty-five years. She is an inspiration in so many ways. Particularly memorable are the glasses of wine in her Toronto home when we share our challenges and I learn much about how organisations and leaders work. She is my close colleague, partner and friend.

I'm especially grateful to my editorial team, who were selected because of their huge contributions to my story. Julia Reed and Judy Benson reviewed my early drafts and provided great insights and structure. Thanks for being part of my life. Larraine Solomon has gone over and above in continuing to keep me on track with her dedication to editing. She has examined the whole manuscript and made it readable ahead of the publication process. I'm grateful for her communication skills, perseverance, support and partnering in our joint ventures. Thanks to my publishing team at Rethink Press, who made the journey of turning the manuscript into a book smooth and supported.

My husband Chris has always supported me reaching my goals and helped me to create the space to have these wonderful experiences, including writing this book.

The Author

Kathryn is a respected and successful strategic change-management consultant with diverse career experience in Europe and North America. She has over twenty-five years of consulting and line experience with leading organisations (Unilever, Mars, KPMG and GSK).

Since 2007, her business has been focusing on partnering with leaders at all levels to drive growth and create sustainable success. For organisations of different sizes, she tailors her approach to develop a better understanding of organisational environment, facilitating strategy workshops and coaching individuals and teams to ensure ideas get implemented. She provides practical and supportive approaches that create focus, accountability and collaboration across organisations and for their partners.

Connect with Kathryn at:

🌐 www.kathrynsimpson.com

🔲 www.linkedin.com/in/kathrynsimpson

🔲 @KathrynESimpson

Printed in Great Britain
by Amazon